MUNI COURT

MUNI COURT

A VIEW FROM THE OTHER SIDE OF THE BENCH

Robert Bluth

iUniverse, Inc.
New York   Bloomington

iUniverse books may be ordered through booksellers or by contacting:

iUniverse
1663 Liberty Drive
Bloomington, IN 47403
www.iuniverse.com
1-800-Authors (1-800-288-4677)

Because of the dynamic nature of the Internet, any Web addresses or links contained in this book may have changed since publication and may no longer be valid. The views expressed in this work are solely those of the author and do not necessarily reflect the views of the publisher, and the publisher hereby disclaims any responsibility for them.

ISBN: 978-1-4401-6494-1 (sc)
ISBN: 978-1-4401-6492-7 (dj)
ISBN: 978-1-4401-6493-4 (ebook)

Printed in the United States of America

iUniverse rev. date: 9/28/2009

Contents

Thanks

Joanie, Barb, Arlene,
Dona, and Paula

Because you were there... .

Introduction

FOR MORE THAN SIXTEEN YEARS, it has been my privilege to serve as a municipal court judge. I am by profession a practicing attorney with almost two decades of general business and litigation experience. The few hours each week that I spend on the other side of the bench help round out my perspective on the judiciary, provides some humorous and entertaining moments and offers insight into the occasional slightly skewed thought processes of the human creature.

If an indiscretion results in a citation to appear in a court in a small community, and if you decide to go to court, you will likely appear before a part-time municipal court judge. Since most people try to avoid citations (a.k.a. tickets), they do not have much experience with the court system. It then follows that most people who appear in court are generally unfamiliar with the forum and are attempting to operate by protocols and rules they do not know, perhaps do not understand, or simply choose to ignore. Those circumstances coupled with the human capacity for creativity and rationalization fuse into a fascinating display of human ingenuity, ineptness, self-rationalization, and much unintended humor as justice is sometimes achieved through unexpected means.

Municipal court is not a court of record; there is no court reporter. The descriptions of the proceedings and quoted conversations are offered as my best recollection of the events that unfolded before the court.

Hell Hath No Fury...

IN SMALL TOWNS WITH LIMITED shopping availability, the grocery store tends to be one of the intersections at which all paths eventually cross. When there is only one place to get disposable diapers, eggs, milk, chips, pop, cigarettes, or beer, the question is not who will be at the store, but when will they be there and whom will they see. For that reason, Murphy (of Murphy's Law fame) dedicates particular attention to this location of infinite possibilities.

Standard evening in court. The parade of unfortunates responds as their names are called. The usual speeding, failure to obey traffic-control device, etc., etc. The next citation has an investigation report attached (not common on traffic citations). Whoa—an Assault III. It is unusual for the officers to cite an assault into muni court. But momentary relief from the mundane is always appreciated. The court also notes that the citation was issued only two days before court.

"Ms. Touché," calls the court.

On the far right of the courtroom, she stands. Age nineteen to twenty one, five feet three, maybe five feet four. Dressed in jeans and boots (western boots of course), stocky but not overweight, broad shoulders, would have made a good linebacker for the Dallas Cowboys. Clean and well-groomed, hair short but well done. Tasteful makeup, soft eyes with a calm, self-assured, confident attitude. She approaches the bench. Stops, faces the court, places both hands on her hips, fingers forward, thumbs back. I note a slight smile; sort of a grin on her face.

"Ms. Touché?" asks the court.

"Yes, Your Honor," she politely responds.

"Ma'am, you are appearing on a citation for Assault III. How do you plead?"

"Guilty, Your Honor," she responds.

"Would you like to tell me what happened?"

"Well, Your Honor," she begins slowly. "I had been going out with this guy for a couple of months. We were just starting to get real serious, you know. That evening I had been talking to him on the phone to see if we could get together. He told me he had to do something at his dad's house but that he would call me later. So I watched TV for a while and then my sister wanted me to take her to the store to get some ice cream. We go to the store and park and, as we are walking up to the door, I see my boyfriend's car. He is in it and this girl is in the passenger seat. I know her. She is a real tramp, if you know what I mean."

At this point, the tone in her voice is getting more, shall we say, more tense.

She continues, "Well, I know what is going on here. So I go over to the car to tell him to go to hell and to tell her what I think of her. When I got to the passenger side of the car, I started to tell them off. She could see I was really mad, and she started to try to roll up the window. So I reached inside to stop her and we were sort of batting each other's hands around when he reached over to try to help her."

She pauses for a moment, then holds her hands out in front of her about waist high as if she were holding a basketball and continues, "His head was right there, you know. Just right there. So I grabbed a hand full of hair on the top of his head, pulled his head out the window and turned his face up a little, and hit him hard in the face three times. Once in the eye, then in his nose, and then I smashed his mouth. I shoved his stupid head back in the window and told him we were through and went in the store with my sister. When we came out, this nice officer (she then points to one of the officers in the courtroom) was waiting for me and gave me this ticket."

Having had her say, Ms. Touché inhales deeply, exhales, and then seems to brace herself for the consequences of her choice in reaction to having been the victim of a cheating, no-good dog. I note the skinned knuckles on her right hand. The tension leaves her body and with a quiet, contented resolve, she awaits the imposition of the sentence.

I take a moment to review the investigation report that confirms her statement. I use the time to collect my thoughts, try to maintain judicial composure, and review her criminal history. No prior arrests or convictions, not even any traffic tickets. A clean record.

"Ma'am," I begin, "you know this kind of behavior is not acceptable and cannot be tolerated"

"Yes, Your Honor," she responds sheepishly.

I then impose the minimum fine and give her sixty days

to get it paid. She politely thanks the court and leaves the courtroom.

I call the name on the next citation and while that matter is being handled, I notice a young couple in the back of the courtroom stand and head toward the door. His left eye is black and swollen and the left side of his mouth has been split and is swollen, but healing. The "victim" and the "tramp." Him I recognize from numerous previous appearances before the court, one of "those." And based solely on "her" appearance … a tramp, to be sure.

Though not acceptable conduct in this society, it seemed to me that in this experience, Ms. Touché won two times: first, she found out what a bum the boyfriend was and, second, the penalty imposed did not outweigh the true satisfaction she got from smashing his cheating face. On some level, in the great quest and pursuit of justice, the balancing of the yin and the yang, Ms. Touché has helped to balance the scales.

My Home, My Castle, My Wheels

ONE CAN ARGUE THE MERITS, **benefits**, infringements on freedom, or inequities of the legislation resulting from the temperance movement. However, it is indisputable that a zealous effort was made to discourage— well … no—more like spank those who insist on driving with a blood-alcohol level above that legislatively defined, yet strongly debated, standard. Traditional temperance sentiments have recently been bolstered by a group of "mad mothers" and supported by an increased awareness of the devastation caused by people operating motor vehicles under the influence of alcohol. Legislators respond well to large blocs of voters, so the laws on the books are extensive, specific, and aimed directly at all aspects of alcohol consumption and all opportunities to consume alcohol. They carry heavy mandatory penalties.

One of my favorites is the "Open Container" law. Basically, if the driver or any of his or her passengers has an open container that has any alcoholic content within their care, custody, or control, or within reasonable reach or access, the driver can be cited. This is an easy law to comply with or even get around in almost all situations if it were not for the fact that most of the culprits are under the influence of alcohol and therefore not coherent enough to put two reasonable thoughts together. Thus, the stage is set. A low hurdle being challenged by a bumbling fool stumbling and thrashing around trying to get over it, while all the time continuing to be his/her own worst enemy.

"Budunwiser" is a late-middle-aged, slender, gaunt-faced, gray-haired, mildly disheveled gentleman with what appears to be a three- to-four-day growth of beard who likely does not commune with warm water and soap on a regular basis. He appears, and with a great deal of fanfare, including a sweeping arm gesture and a slight bow at the waist as he introduces himself to the court. Of course, he entered a not-guilty plea to the citation for open container. As the court attempts to advise him to appear for trial on the scheduled date, the *odeur d'* alcohol overpowers the olfactory organs of everyone within twenty feet him. The officer who wrote the citation stands in the back of the courtroom, shaking his head in disbelief and grinning.

Time passes. A couple of weeks later it's time for the trial. We have saved this case for the last to minimize the size of the audience to witness the fiasco that we expect to unfold. The court calls the case: *The city v. Mr. Budunwiser*. The officer and Budunwiser approach the bench. The officer is poised and ready, composed and confident; Budunwiser is righteously indignant and swaying while standing with his feet spread wide apart.

"Is the city ready to proceed?"

"Yes, Your Honor," responds the officer crisply.

"Mr. Budunwiser, are you ready to proceed?"

"Yes, Your Honor." Once again, the sweeping arm gesture and the bow and returning to what appears to an uncomfortable pose. Chin elevated and extended, eyes bloodshot and trying to focus. Dramatic.

The officer is sworn in and proceeds: "On blankety-blank date while on duty in the city, in a marked patrol car, in full uniform, badge prominently displayed, I observed a conversion van weaving within its lane of travel. As I caught up with the vehicle, it pulled off the road in front of an auto-repair shop. I noted that there was no right turn signal for the turn and when the vehicle came to a stop, the right brake light did not come on. I made contact with the driver and identified him as Mr. Budunwiser from his driver's license. As I approached the driver's window, there was a strong odor of alcohol emanating from the vehicle. I noticed a glass of liquid in the cup holder in the center console that appeared to be wine. Upon further examination, I smelled it, and it was determined to be wine. The vehicle was impounded due to Budunwiser's failure of field sobriety tests, and while inventorying the vehicle I located an open, partially filled bottle of wine at the back of the center console and well within reach of the driver. I cited Budunwiser into this court on the open-container citation."

"Mr. Budunwiser, do you have questions for the officer on anything he said? This is your opportunity for cross-examination."

Mr. Budunwiser ponders for a moment, composes himself, and blurts out, "Yes, Your Honor, I do. How can you … you know … you are lying … Hummmm, well, it's not right that you come in here and lie like that …."

The court interrupts, "Mr. Budunwiser, it appears that you are going to testify as to what happened. Why don't we put you under oath so you can just tell me what happened?" The stench of alcohol has engulfed the entire courtroom by now. Budunwiser's speech is slurred and deliberate, and his eyes are blinking. Standing still is not within his ability as the swaying continues and becomes more pronounced. This will be interesting. One wonders, had he used alcohol to muster courage to appear, or was this the result of a spontaneous celebration, or more likely, the most common state of being for Budunwiser? The court asks Budunwiser to raise his right hand and acknowledge the oath and then asks Budunwiser to proceed.

He inhales deeply and begins, "I write music, beautiful music. (Relevance to the issues at hand? Unknown. But one never knows and must give the defendants every opportunity in their defense.) I had driven up to a place in the mountains that I found a while back with my son. It is a beautiful place, quiet and nice and a … a … a … a … inspirational for me. Yes, I did have a glass of wine. I was writing a new score or something, it was really going well. I do write beautiful music. And, well, later, sometime later, I got out and walked around in the woods. Then when I got back in my van I discovered that the door things, you know, a … a … a … a … all the things on the door did not work. It is the, the, the, locks, yeah, the locks and the thing that makes it go up and down, the thing, a … a … a … the glass thing, a … a …"

"The window?"

"Yeah, the window, none of it would work. So I got out and checked the van and the taillight on the right side was not working either. So, I am very conscious … conscious … conscientious and careful to take care of my van. I came back into town to see my good friend who runs the auto shop to get the van fixed. I had just pulled off at my good friend's shop when this officer pulled up behind me. Your Honor, are you responsible for how these officers are trained?"

"No, Mr. Budunwiser, that would be the chief's job."

"This officer was very rude to me, rude and arrogant, and …"

"Mr. Budunwiser, why don't you just tell me what happened in regards to the open-container citation."

"Well, OK, there we are in front of my good friend's place and this officer has me doing all these tests, which don't make any sense to me, and he asked me what is in the glass in my van. I tell him it is wine from a long time ago this morning when I was up in the mountains writing music, like I told you. I told him I want to have my good friend fix my van. Your Honor, can I ask you a question?"

"Go ahead, sir."

"Thank you." (The sweeping arm gesture and the bow again. Cool, huh?) "Is it not true, Your Honor, that it is not against the law to drink a glass of wine in your home?"

"The court would agree with that general proposition."

"Well, at that particular time I was living in my van and considered it to be my home. And it is not against the law to drink a little wine in your home. So, this ticket should be dismissed."

"Mr. Budunwiser, how about the bottle of wine found by the console in your van?"

"I keep my wine in my home with me."

"Where do you live when you are not living in your van? What address is on your driver's license?"

"I live with my son most of the time. Just sometimes, I consider myself to be living in my van."

"OK. How long had you been living in your van on the day when you got this ticket?"

"All that day."

"And where were you going to spend the night that night?"

"Oh, back at my son's house."

"So, you were just considering yourself to be living in your van for the day?"

"Well, I had not really decided at that point for how long."

"OK, anything else you would like me to consider?"

"No, that's pretty much it."

"Based on the evidence before me, I will find you guilty on the citation as charged. Despite the novelty of your defense, I will impose the minimum fine of $___. Can you pay that now, or do you need to make payments?"

"That's not right, I don't see ..."

"Mr. Budunwiser, this no longer the time for discussion on the matter. I only need to know if you can pay the fine or if you need to make payments."

"This is not fair. I am on disability. I only get $549 a month. I have a lot of bills to pay also. I can't make any payments hardly. I pay a lot of things. I pay my son $350 a month for rent, I pay $85 a month for insurance, I pay $40 and $60 something for medical coverage and over a $100 a month for prescriptions. I got to buy gas and food and clothes ..."

He goes on and on and on. Drunks under the influence, knowing that they are under the influence of alcohol, tend to overcompensate. By so doing, usually they are their own worst enemies. A payment schedule is set and specific instructions are given, although I am certain they will not be remembered, at least not accurately, by the next moment of sobriety. Yes, I can do the math as to Budunwiser's income versus his payments. And while I am tempted to ask for an explanation of how Budunwiser is able to pay for over $635 of bills with $549, it is not likely that Budunwiser can explain or that I will be able to understand any explanation offered. We will just have to save that for another day.

To Err Is Human; To Avoid the Consequences—Well, That Would Be the Challenge

Most cases come before the court for only one appearance: for arraignment. They plead guilty. We do the fine thing. They pay within thirty days or there is a payment plan. Justice is satisfied. Life returns to normal, and the world moves on.

A not-guilty plea requires at least a second appearance for the trial and, if the defendant is found guilty, once again we do the fine thing and he/she pays within thirty days or on a payment plan. If there is a not-guilty finding by the court, of course, we skip that whole fine thing. That is the average case. However, some cases are not average. Some cases tend to create a life of their own. Some cases you cannot seem to get resolved even if you could beat them with a stick.

Some cases go on and on, but they are just plain interesting. As these types of cases unfold, we are just waiting to see what the next chapter will be. This case was one of those.

Mr. Shuckin, (as in shuck'n and jiv'n) needs some

discussion and description before we get into the facts and events that follow. Mr. Shuckin is a young man. Just over eighteen years of age. Large, six feet two or so. Round everything, round face, round waist, round arms, round legs. Like I said, Shuckin is round. Shuckin is the kind of person who has managed to keep girth ahead of vertical growth. Very pleasing personality, very personable. He has avoided most of life's responsibilities by smooth-talking or sweet-talking or just plain shoveling bovine dung. His gift of gab has managed to get most folks to like him and let him off the hook time after time after time, and again and again and again and again. An intelligent kid, but the lack of diligence in education is reflected in his redneck vocabulary and his presentation is compensated for with "aw shucks, gee golly darn" and "life has been tough for me" explanations. From the first time he appears in front of the court, I genuinely like him.

Early in the docket on a Wednesday evening, the courtroom is still crowded; seats are all full with some people still standing. The court calls the case: "Mr. Shuckin."

He stands immediately. He is in the middle of the back row, of course, and has a big friendly smile on his face. Immediately the stream of chatter begins.

"I am here, Your Honor. I will be right there. I did not know you would call me so soon or I would have stood up closer to the front."

While the stream of chatter continues, he is making his way to the end of the back row. By the expression on the faces of the people he is passing, it is obvious that in his haste he is stepping on feet, bumping into legs, and brushing and bumping the backs of the heads of the people in the next-to-last row. And the chatter continues. Finally, he explodes through the crowd and approaches the bench. He stops, puts both his hands on his hips. The chatter stops long enough for him to inhale, and with a big smile he blurts out, "How are you this evening, Your Honor?"

There are a couple of seconds of silence as the universe realigns itself and the world readjusts. And we are ready to continue.

"I am just fine this evening, Mr. Shuckin. Thank you for asking. How are you?"

"I am doing OK, I hope," he responds.

"Mr. Shuckin, you are appearing on two citations, one for speeding and one for failing to have your driver's license with you. How do you plead?"

"Well, I was not going as fast as the officer put on the ticket, but I probably was speeding just a little, so I guess I will plead, oohh, hummm, I guess … probably … guilty. Oh, yeah, I did not have my license with me so I'm definitely guilty on that one."

With the entry of guilty pleas, the court then reviews the driving record, nothing big or out of the ordinary. With some concern for the likely onslaught of chatter that will certainly follow, I offer an opportunity for an explanation.

"Would you like to tell me why you were speeding or what was going on at the time?"

"Well, Your Honor, I was late to where I was going, so I was trying to get there as fast as I could and in the rush I forgot to put my wallet in my pocket before I left home."

"Very well, thank you for the brief explanation."

Mr. Shuckin beams proudly as if he has done the world a

favor. So, the court goes on with imposing minimum statutory fines on both charges and sets up a payment schedule of $50 a month and a schedule for the payments. At this point, I think the case is over. But no. The fates have not designated this to be the end. In fact, it is only the beginning.

Then, the one and only time this has ever happened, a woman stands, raises her hand to get my attention. Believe it or … well, just believe it.

"Your Honor, Your Honor, may I say something?"

"Who are you, ma'am?"

"I am Mr. Shuckin's stepmother. His father and I would like to know if you could put him in jail, even if it is for just a couple of days. We think it would do him a lot of good."

The crowd bursts into laughter. Mr. Shuckin is still facing the bench, head down, blushing, beet red, and shaking his head in disbelief. After the reality of what has just happened settles in, I realize that the woman is not joking. The request has been made with earnest intent.

When quiet has returned to the courtroom, she continues, "He is not a bad kid. He just needs to do some growing up. He seems to always be able to talk his way out of everything he gets himself into. So, I am glad you at least hit him with a good fine. But if he doesn't change what he's doing, he is going to get into real trouble. His Dad and I think that if he could see what it is like in jail it would help him to straighten out some."

"Well, ma'am, at this point, I cannot send him to jail. I would like to accommodate your request. But as I explained to him, if he doesn't make the payments as scheduled or appear in court, I will issue a warrant and he will get to go to jail. Mr.

Shuckin, with that request from your parents, you can rest assured that the first time you blow it, I will have you lodged in jail. And ma'am, if you are correct about his personality and his character, that probably will not take too long. So, Mr. Shuckin, remember that that first payment is due here by the date scheduled or you will need to be back here in court. Are we clear on that point? I have got to be honest with you. It would be my pleasure to be able to comply with your parents' request."

"No, Your Honor, she's not my mom. She is my stepmom," he said with some disdain, rolling his eyes and continuing to shake his head.

"That would be a distinction without a difference. Mother or stepmother, I will treat the request as coming from a caring parent. That will be all for now. Just make real sure you make those payments."

Time marches on. The date for Mr. Shuckin's first payment comes and goes. No payment, but he does appear in court that night. I notice him standing to the side, and he is quite fidgety. Seems like he is in a hurry to leave. As the court is proceeding through the docket of new citations, Mr. Shuckin waits for the conclusion of a case and then interrupts the court.

"Your Honor, I have somewhere I need to be. Could I talk to you now?"

"No, Mr. Shuckin. Everyone here has somewhere they would rather be or need to be also. You will have to wait your turn."

We finish the new citations and get to the "pay or appear" group and eventually get to Mr. Shuckin.

As his name is called, he rushes to the bench, obviously irritated and in a hurry. The big smiled is replaced with a stern and concerned look. Not angry, more like concerned.

"Mr. Shuckin, you have not made your payment as scheduled, but you are here. Why haven't you made that payment?"

"Well, I do not have the money right now, but I will get you paid. Your Honor, I am afraid I won't be able to come to court on Wednesday night like this for a while. Do you have court at any other time?"

"No. Wednesday night is the scheduled court time. You will need to appear on Wednesday evening unless you make those payments."

"I won't be able to do that."

"Why not? What else is happening on Wednesday evening?"

"Since I was here last, I have started going to church. I am trying to get my life together. It has been helping me a lot, and the minister has Bible study on Wednesdays at the same time as you have court. My minister says it is really important that I be at the Bible study group, and I think it will help me a lot so I have to be there. By making me come here tonight you have made me late for Bible study and by now I have probably missed the whole thing."

A snicker rumbles through the audience of regular attendees.

"That is a problem now, isn't it? Mr. Shuckin, will the minister issue a warrant and have you lodged in jail if you do not make it to Bible study?"

"No, sir. He is a minister. He is a real nice person who is trying to help me."

"Well, Mr. Shuckin, when you are setting up your itinerary for Wednesday nights, you should consider the fact that I will issue a warrant if you do not appear in this court as scheduled. On the other hand, you can always make that payment and not have to come to court on Wednesday. Then you would be able to go to Bible study without the problem of a warrant being issued for your arrest."

"I just don't have the money to make the payments. I have a lot of bills, and I only work part-time. I am having a tough time right now."

"If you have not made your payment by the next court date, you will need to be here. Are we clear on that?"

Head shaking in disbelief and a concerned look on his face, he leaves in a rush, purportedly on his way to Bible study. The court has some real doubts as to the sincerity of the sudden conversion to and dedication to the divine. I also would not bet my last dollar that when he leaves he will go to Bible study. But one can always hope and pray that the professed dedication is followed through on and will result in a more responsible, better Mr. Shuckin, emerging reborn and renewed from his commitment to the faith. One must remain optimistic and open even to the infinitely remote possibility.

The next court date arrives, but neither a payment nor Mr. Shuckin are present. The clerk is requested to send Mr. Shuckin a letter, reminding him of his obligation to the court and giving him one more chance to pay or appear before a warrant is issued. The next court date arrives and, once again, no payment and no Mr. Shuckin. A warrant is issued.

A few weeks go by. As court begins on a Wednesday night, there in the audience is Mr. Shuckin. When we get to Mr. Shuckin, I review his file and there is a release form from a county jail. Not our local county jail, a neighboring county jail on the coast. Mr. Shuckin has been lodged in jail and released on a citation to appear in this court tonight.

"Mr. Shuckin," calls the court. He approaches the bench somewhat contrite. And the court continues, "It appears that we, and that 'we' would be you, me, the clerks, a police officer, and a jailer, have been able to fulfill your parents' request. You got to go to jail. And it was not here in our friendly county. You were over on the coast. Were you on vacation or doing something fun over there?"

"It was terrible! Your Honor, I got married last Friday afternoon. I got off work at noon, and my fiancée and I went down to the county courthouse and got married. After we got married, we were going to the coast for our honeymoon for the weekend. See, I had to be back to work on Monday morning. Just as we were driving into town on the coast, I got pulled over by a police officer. He said that the little light that lights up the license plate was not working and he was going to tell me so I could get it fixed. But when he ran me through the computer, it came back that there was a warrant from you for my arrest. He put me in jail! Can you believe it? I did not get out until Monday morning. My wife spent the weekend in the hotel alone. She spent our honeymoon alone. She picked me up at the courthouse after the judge let me go and by the time I got back here I was real late for work. Because I was late, I got fired from my job. So, I spent my honeymoon in jail and lost my job because of your warrant."

The audience in the courtroom bursts into laughter. After that recitation of events, I just have to let it sink in for a moment. Struggling to keep from laughing and trying to maintain some decorum, I wait for the laughter to subside.

"You know, Mr. Shuckin, sometimes, without my even trying, fate just steps in and kind of helps us out. I intentionally try to arrange consequences to encourage compliance with court obligations and civic responsibilities. But on my best day, I could not have arranged all that for you even if I had tried. You can only imagine the pride I feel by having been able to fulfill your stepmother's most earnest request. Now, have I convinced you that I am serious about you following through and taking care of your obligation to the city?"

What follows is a long diatribe of tales of woe, unfortunate circumstances, pleas for pity, now married, financial respon-sibilities, etc., etc., etc. Basically, the standard "if you can't dazzle them with brilliance, baffle them with BS." Although the entire speech is presented with grand gestures, a furrowed brow, as much sincerity as could be mustered, and a lot of sucking up to the court, it has the depth of a child's wading pool and the sincerity of a door-to-door encyclopedia sales-man.

"Mr. Shuckin, let me make this real simple for you. You make a payment by the next court date or be here in court. Your own death would be an acceptable excuse and then only if someone presents a death certificate that can be verified. Are you clear on this?"

"Oh, yes, Your Honor, I will be here, you can ..." And the litany continues. Eventually, as he pauses to inhale a breath of fresh air, I call the next case and court moves forward.

The next court date, there he is, seated in the front row. Smiling so big one would assume (erroneously) that a significant event has occurred or is about to occur. Mr. Shuckin makes comments to those seated around him on each and every case during court until his turn comes on the docket. Mr. Shuckin has become the newest self-proclaimed expert on the law and court procedure. When his name is called early in the docket, he begins, "I am here, Your Honor (like everyone in the courtroom was not already aware of that), just like you told me to be. You are looking good this evening. It is really interesting to watch court. I think this is going to be kind of fun. I am learning a lot about court, the law, the police, and these people. I am not working and do not have any money. It has been quite a while since you fined me and I went to jail and all, so why don't we just call it even, you know, and let bygones be bygones?"

"Are you expecting me to dismiss your ticket?"

"Don't ya think that would be fair? I mean, I spent my honeymoon in jail. That's pretty harsh for a traffic ticket, don't you think?"

"Well, Mr. Shuckin, if not for your mother's request ... No, that is not true, I would not consider that even if your mother had not requested that I put you in jail. Besides, if your mother thinks that going to jail once would help, maybe going more than once, say twice or three times, would help even more."

"She is my stepmom, not my real mother."

"A point on which I am sure she finds great comfort and personal relief. However, your only option in this court is to pay the fine. The fine is small by comparison to other fines, but with the additional warrant fees, it is starting to grow. How is your stepmom?"

"She is not here to enjoy the way you are making me suffer. She is in Mexico."

"Well, Mr. Shuckin, since you are enjoying this court experience so much and have much more you want to say, why don't you have a seat back there and you can wait until the end of the docket to discuss you case. The rest of these people do not need to wait while you and I discuss your case"

"But, Your Honor, I really need to be going."

"Mr. Shuckin, it is difficult for me to track whether you are going, want to stay, don't want to stay, have something to say, are done having your say. My, but you are fickle. You have a seat and wait."

Court continues on with the docket. Mr. Shuckin is bouncing from cheek to cheek, sighing deeply and loudly, looking at the clock, and rolling his eyes. Surprisingly, by the time we get to end of the docket, Mr. Shuckin has nothing left to say. I remind Mr. Shuckin that he needs to make his payment or appear in court at the next court date. He acknowledges the date and hastily disappears into the night.

Over the next several months, there are regular appearances by Mr. Shuckin, but he misses again, so more warrants are issued and he is lodged in jail several times.

*   *   *

On this particular night, Mr. Shuckin is present. The court receives notice from the jail that Mr. Shuckin has been lodged again and released on an order to appear in court.

"Mr. Shuckin, I note from the record that you got to go to jail again. If you keep this up, your stepmother will be ecstatic with me."

"I don't know how you do it, Your Honor. Last Saturday, I am hanging around the house, relaxing. It was my wife's and my first anniversary. We have plans to celebrate our first anniversary since you spoiled our honeymoon. Just as we are ready to go out, there is a knock on the door. So I answer it. It's the cops. They take me to jail, and I spend the weekend in jail and miss my anniversary. Do you plan these things that way?"

"I would be proud to be able to claim that I knew or remembered or even cared when your anniversary was. I am lucky to remember my own anniversary. But I admit if I had thought of it, I likely would have made an attempt to do that. But that does beg the question: am I going to have an opportunity to have to lodge you on your second anniversary?"

"Not a chance. I am going to take care of this. I going to come to court with the full payment in one-dollar bills and make you count them."

"If you notify the court when you will be bringing the full payment in, the court will consider providing cake and punch for the occasion. We'll count the money, have some cake and wish you a great life. However, just in case you do not happen to have the full amount, you can still make the scheduled payment before next court or … How do we finish this sentence?"

"Be in court or you will issue a warrant, yeah, yeah, I know, I know."

Months go by, Mr. Shuckin continues to appear, miss, get lodged in jail. This looks like it will become the cycle of life. No, more like the cycle of the lack of life that goes on and on. Still no payments.

*   *   *

One day, I am in the downtown of the city I live in, which is not either of the cities where I serve as municipal court judge. It is a small city. I am on my way to a small sandwich shop for lunch. Just as I am approaching the shop, from the opposite direction I see Mr. Shuckin coming in my direction, moving at a hurried pace. I note money in his hand. True confession time: my first thought is that Mr. Shuckin has just stolen some poor old lady's money. He sees me. Recognizes me and comes to an abrupt stop.

"Your Honor, what are you doing here?"

"Mr. Shuckin, it may come as a surprise to you, but somewhere around the middle of each day, I consume food. I call it lunch."

"Haahaa, very good. Very good. My boss sent me to pick up sandwiches. I got to hurry."

"By all means, hurry. I would not interfere with a working man."

It is good to see Mr. Shuckin engaged in a worthwhile endeavor. For a few weeks, I hold out on an optimistic dream that maybe Mr. Shuckin has turned a corner and is heading toward responsibility and success. But time goes on, and he gets lodged several more times. On one occasion after being lodged, he appears in court. When we get to his turn on the docket, he approaches, puts his hands on his hips, assumes a concerned appearance, and begins:

"Your Honor, this is getting embarrassing."

"For whom is this getting embarrassing, Mr. Shuckin?"

"Well, Your Honor, last Saturday, I was at home. The cops come to my house. They know where I live, they have been there so much. They knock on the door and when my four-year-old son sees them he says, 'They're not going to take you to jail again, are they?' Then I had to explain that yes, they were going to take me to jail again because I still have not paid the ticket off. Then he says, 'Why don't you just pay the ticket, Dad?'"

"That is fascinating, Mr. Shuckin. Let me see if I have got this straight. Your four-year-old son has figured this whole thing out. Pay the ticket and you don't have to go to jail. And after all this time, you still have not figured that out. What is going on here? Are you sure that he is your son, or was there a genetic mutation on intellectual capability? You should listen to your son, Mr. Shuckin. You don't seem to be listening to me or your stepmom."

"Well ... well ... well ... I am going to get this thing behind me. And when I do, I am never coming back to this stinking town."

"Mr. Shuckin, you and any other law-abiding citizen are welcome here any time. You may want to note on your way out of town tonight that there are lots and lots of people who live here, hundreds, thousands, even. They like this community and have never met me."

"They don't know you?"

"Nope, never been in this courtroom. They actually get

driver's licenses, insurance, they obey the law. They enjoy the parks and wonderful accommodations that this fair city has to offer. You, too, are welcome. Bring your wife, your son; come for a visit. In fact, I would like to meet the bright young man."

"Not likely ..."

And with that, next court date is scheduled and Mr. Shuckin is off and on his way.

I would like to tell you that Mr. Shuckin cleared up his issues and moved on to a good and productive life, but I cannot. Mr. Shuckin was lodged several more times. Time, unstoppable time, moves on. And at least some things yield to time and persistence.

*   *   *

Time passes on. Mr. Shuckin appears on a court night without having been lodged in jail. An attractive young lady is with him, presumably the long-suffering wife. Shuckin has a "cat that has eaten the canary" look on his face and cannot wait for his name to be called. Finally, he is up at bat.

"Mr. Shuckin, good to see you here this evening. Is that your wife with you?"

"Yes, Your Honor, it is."

"So, Mr. Shuckin, you are appearing instead of making a payment?"

"No sir, Your Honor. Do you have the cake and punch ready?"

"No, I do not. You did not give me any advanced notice of the need for cake and punch. And obviously, it would have been impossible for me to anticipate this possibly momentous occasion. You have brought money with you to court this evening?"

He reaches in his pocket and takes out a significant roll of bills. Holds them up proudly and says, "I have got money right here. How about I give you all of this money and we just call it even?"

"Well, that would depend on how much money is there. If that is all hundred-dollar bills, that is probably too much, but we can probably work that out. If it is all one-dollar bills, that is not likely to be enough."

He grins, "Why don't you just take a chance? You come out ahead."

"The court has no interest in 'coming out ahead.' Correct payment of fine is our goal here. How much do you have there? Better yet, why don't you just start counting money and when you get to the amount you owe, I will stop you."

And he begins count bills. They are all one-dollar bills. Mr. Shuckin counts them in stacks of ten, arranging the stacks in a neat row in front of him. There is only enough for about half of his fine. When he finishes, he looks up at me, proud at what he has done.

"There you go, Your Honor, that's all I have right now."

"That is a good start, Mr. Shuckin. However, it will take more to meet your obligation to the city. I will, however, dismiss some of the warrant fees in exchange for another large payment."

Mr. Shuckin asks for a firm amount and promises to return in two weeks with the remaining balance, all in one-dollar bills.

Two weeks go by. Mr. Shuckin is back. Once again, with a

roll of one-dollar bills. We do the counting exercise again, and his fine is paid in full. I regret that I did not believe him when he said he would return so I could have at least had some cake for him to commemorate the occasion. But his past record did not warrant risking the loss of good cake just on the chance he might follow through. Though the pleasant surprise satiated any sense of loss for the missed opportunity.

I have not seen Mr. Shuckin since then. His stepmother and father were correct. Some jail time did seem to help him grow up some.

Mama's Little Girl
Done Grow'd Up

A SIGNIFICANT NUMBER OF PATRONS OF the court are younger people in the eighteen- to-twenty-five age range. The reasons for their appearing, while varied, are the same issues and citations that burden the broader population. One particular young man, however, was a unique experience. Mr. Unique was attempting to be a disenfranchised member of the broader society while being the center of his own universe. Sort of a countercultural, evangelical, self-appointed movement of one person.

Mr. Unique was a slender young man, quiet, soft-spoken, dark shaggy hair, dark yet soft eyes that were frequently bloodshot. He was a dedicated skateboarder with a long history with the court, having been cited and convicted on many charges. He had dropped out of high school in the early grades and spent his time skateboarding and hanging out down by the bridge, expounding philosophy. Philosophy that he had mostly contemplated, contrived, or conjured up while under the influence of, or with the aid of, a vegetative matter that is illegal to smoke or sell. From time to time, he had an entourage accompanying him. The entire group had the sartorial look of having shopped at the store for big and tall men even though the tallest and biggest of the group was a solid five feet six inches tall and weighed one hundred fifty pounds. The females of the entourage, well, let's say, it is good to have a group that you fit in with.

Mr. Unique had never been rude or threatening to the court. To the contrary, he was always soft-spoken and respectful. In fact, his integrity was quite high. When charged with a matter for which he believed he was guilty, he always pled guilty and took his lumps. He was not quite that strong on following through on the payment of the fines. Unfortunately, skateboarding, loitering, and philosophizing had never been financially rewarding for him. That, coupled with the lack of a real job, created cash-flow issues that were an ongoing struggle for Mr. Unique.

When Mr. Unique appeared, skateboard tucked under his arm, on a citation for trespassing, he smiled at me and said, "Your Honor, you know me. I have always been straight with you. I am going to enter a not-guilty plea on this one because I am not guilty. I know that you will set the matter for trial and you do not have an address for me, so when your clerk (and he called her by name) has the notice ready, you can have an officer just find me. I am usually down by the bridge. I will be glad to appear at court. Besides, being as I cannot make payments, I am generally here at court every time anyway."

With that long explanation, he politely nodded his head and departed from the courtroom. I was not sure what the facts and circumstances were going to be at the trial, but I was willing to bet that it was going to be interesting. Mr. Unique never does anything halfway. When he gets into trouble, he does it in a big sort of way with a lot of flare.

Trial is set and the case is called. "Mr. Unique, are you ready to proceed?"

"Yes, Your Honor, I am ready to proceed."

"Very well, sir. Officer, is the city ready to proceed?"

"Yes, I am, Your Honor. Your Honor, this is a citizen-signed citation and the citizen is present in the court and will testify."

"Very well. Raise your right hand and be sworn."

Whereupon, the officer is sworn in and begins to testify.

"Your Honor, I was on duty in the city on blankety-blank day at about two thirty in the morning when I received a call from dispatch that directed me to a particular address. I went to that address, which I know to be the residence of Mrs. Complainer. Upon arrival at the residence, Mrs. Complainer meets me in the front yard and tells me that Mr. Unique has trespassed on her property. She advises me that she told Mr. Unique not to come back on her property and that she had found Mr. Unique in her house. She further advised that when she screamed at Mr. Unique to get out that he had run out through the yard, down the alley, and disappeared into the night. I filled out the citation for trespassing. Mrs. Complainer signed the citation. The following day I found Mr. Unique at his usual haunt down by the bridge and served the citation on him at that time. At this time, Your Honor, I have nothing further to say being as I did not witness any of the events and would therefore call Mrs. Complainer to testify."

"Thank you, Officer, but before we move on to Mrs. Complainer, let's make sure that Mr. Unique does not have any questions on cross-examination for you. Mr. Unique, do you have any questions for the officer?"

"No, Your Honor, I do not. What he said was exactly what happened."

"Very well. Mrs. Complainer, can you come forward and be sworn."

Whereupon, the witness is sworn in and the court continues.

"Can you tell me what happened?"

"Your Honor, Mr. Unique was my daughter's boyfriend. He is a couple of years older than her and he is no good for her. He used to come over to my house at all times of the day and night. Two days before this night, I came home and found him in the living room with my daughter. I told him then he had better get out of my house and he better never come back. If he ever came back, I told him I would call the police and have him thrown in jail for trespassing. I do not want him around my daughter. I do not want him in my house." Although she began relatively calm and collected, with each word the emotion and anger is building.

"Mrs. Complainer, I need you to tell me what happened on the night the citation was issued."

She inhales deeply and continues, "On the night that the citation was issued, I had been out with my boyfriend. When I got in, it was well after midnight. It was really late, and Mr. Unique was in my house. I screamed at him, and he ran out of the house. I saw him run down the alley. I could not see where he went after that. I called 911 and they sent the officer over right away."

"Very well. Mr. Unique, do you have any questions of this witness?"

Mr. Unique kind of smiles at me and says, "Yes, Your Honor, I have a couple of questions. Mrs. Complainer, I was in your daughter's bedroom when you came home, wasn't I?"

The courtroom goes totally silent. There is a silent pause of several seconds. Mrs. Complainer is now really tense and rigid. Her face goes through several increasing shades of red, ending in something like crimson. Finally she responds without looking at Mr. Unique.

"Yes, you were."

He continues, "When you screamed at me, I had to put some clothes on and jump out the window, didn't I?"

Once again, there is a long, silent pause, and the tension is rising in the courtroom. The police officers sense the tension, and one of them moves into position behind the two people in front of me. Mrs. Complainer now has her teeth tightly clenched and with her jaw not moving responds, "That's right."

"That is all I have now, Your Honor."

"Anything further, Officer or Mrs. Complainer?"

"No," says the officer trying not to smile.

"No!" says Mrs. Complainer emphatically.

"Mrs. Complainer, thank you."

I wait a few seconds to let the drama and tension recede and then continue.

"Very well. Mr. Unique, raise your right hand and be sworn. Do you …"

Unable to contain himself, Mr. Unique interrupts me and begins, "Your Honor, I was over at a friend's house earlier that evening, and I was talking on the phone to Mrs. Complainer's daughter."

Seated in the courtroom in a chair next to the seat where Mrs. Complainer has been seated is a young woman who returns a smile to Mr. Unique as he looks back at her.

Mr. Unique continues, "Mrs. Complainer's daughter used to be my girlfriend until just a couple days ago when we broke up. So when I was at my friend's house, I started talking to her on the phone. She told me to come over. I told her that her mother told me I could not come over there a couple of days before. She said she knew that but that her mother was going to be leaving pretty soon and that I should come over there right then. I told her that I did not want to get her into any trouble. She said that was fine, that she lived there too, and that she paid part of the rent, and that she could have anybody over that she wanted. So I went down the alley and walked through the backyard like she told me to and knocked on her bedroom window. She opened her bedroom window and helped pull me into her bedroom through her window. I got there before her mother went out earlier in the evening. I had been there with her daughter all the time her mother had been out. In fact, part of the time we had been out in the living room watching some TV. When we heard her mother come home, we ran back into the bedroom and her mother came in and saw me and just went crazy. She started screaming at me and trying to throw things at me, so I put my pants on real quick, grabbed the rest of my stuff, and just dove out the window. I jumped up and ran down the alley. Your Honor, I do not think I was trespassing because I was invited to come over there. Someone told me I could come. I went down to the library and looked up trespassing. I do not think I was trespassing. Your Honor, I would like to call a witness and that would be Mrs. Complainer's daughter."

At this point, the use of some judicial discretion seems in order. There is a situation about to escalate here that will not be pretty if it explodes in front of me. Mrs. Complainer is bright red, eyes squinted, teeth clenched, and the visual image of a partially clad Mr. Unique jumping out of her daughter's bedroom window has now reentered her conscious memory. The whole incident is so distasteful to her that it has angered her to such a level that she is about to lose it. Furthermore, I do not know that it is the court's job or mission to create a conflict between mothers and daughters. Therefore, in an attempt to diffuse the situation, I call Mrs. Complainer's daughter to approach the bench, way off to the side by the police officer.

When she is there, I begin. "You have been sitting in the courtroom and you heard your mother's testimony."

With a sheepish grin on her face and a slight smile hidden behind her hand so her mother cannot see, she says, "Yes, Your Honor, I did."

"You have also heard Mr. Unique recite his version of what happened."

There is an audible chortle of laughter that ripples through the audience. The daughter turns around and looks at a friend who is with her, giggles slightly, and looks back at the court and says, "Yes, Your Honor, I heard that. I heard it all."

"If you were to testify under oath, would your testimony differ in any material respect from anything you have heard by the prior two witnesses?"

"No, Your Honor, I do not think it would."

"Very well, you may be seated. Mr. Unique, is there anything else you would like the court to consider?"

"No, Your Honor, that is about it." There is a slight smile on Mr. Unique's face as he fights the urge to explode into laughter. The officers and clerks are in the same mode of self-restraint. I, on the other hand, am calm and composed, at least on the outside.

"Very well. Mrs. Complainer, is there any other evidence you would like the court to consider?"

"No, Your Honor, there is not," she says sternly, now glaring at Mr. Unique.

If looks could kill, Mr. Unique would be dead, or at least injured to where he would suffer greatly.

"Very well. Based on the evidence before the court, I find that the city and the complainant have not met the burden of proof to establish trespass as charged. Therefore, this citation will be dismissed. However, Mr. Unique, please have a seat over in the courtroom. You are to remain in the courtroom until released by the court. Do you understand that?"

Mr. Unique smiles broadly, "Yes, Your Honor, I do understand that, and I will be glad to sit over there until you tell me I can go."

The court then turns to Mrs. Complainer, "You are now free to leave the courtroom, and I would advise you to do so. I also want to advise you that you should not undertake any action on your own in regard to this situation. If you would politely and quietly leave the court right now, the court would appreciate your cooperation on this matter."

The invitation to leave the court was a waste of time and

breath. By the time the words were out of my mouth, she had already turned and was storming toward the exit door. Her daughter sat where she had been for a good ten seconds after her mother left the courtroom. Then the daughter smiled and waved at Mr. Unique and, with her friend, quietly left the courtroom.

About a half hour later, when court was done, I advised Mr. Unique that he was free to leave the courtroom, hoping that enough time had passed and distance had been created between Mrs. Complainer and him that it would give him at least a running start if Mrs. Complainer did not follow the court's advice and decided to take things into her hands.

What Friends Are For

THE INTRODUCTION OF EVIDENCE IN a case is followed by the sifting and then the weighing of the evidence. Woo! Sounds complex and sometimes can be. The touchstone, from the Court's perspective, is that the defendant is not guilty until and unless so proven. And that proof must be to a moral certainty beyond a reasonable doubt. Thus, if I have a question, a doubt, a significant degree of uncertainty, the case has not been proven and dismissal is mandated. Cool legal-jargon stuff, huh?

Fortunately, in most cases where a factual determination between conflicting statements is necessary, there is a point, a watershed event, an epiphany, if you will, which becomes the lens through which clarity of vision and understanding allows for a decision to be made with a comfortable level of confidence.

The facts of this case: a speeding ticket, a not-guilty plea—trial is set and the officer must present his case.

"On blankety-blank date, at two fifteen in the afternoon, I was on duty as an officer for the city. I was in a marked patrol car, in uniform, badge prominently displayed. While conducting radar surveillance on Central Avenue, I saw a vehicle approaching at a high rate of speed. I activated the radar and clocked the speed of the oncoming car at forty-seven miles per hour in a posted thirty-five-mile-per-hour zone. I am trained in the operation of radar and the radar had been tested prior to my shift and at the end of my shift that day and was found to be functioning properly. As the vehicle went past me, I activated the lights and pursued the vehicle. As I caught up with the vehicle, the vehicle pulled over to the shoulder in the nine-hundred block of West Named Street. I approached the vehicle, identified the driver as Mr. Ordinary by his driver's license, and issued him a citation for speeding."

Mr. Ordinary, the defendant, twenty-five to thirty years of age, average in appearance, cleaned up for court. A lot of head shaking and looks of astonishment and disbelief thoughout the officer's testimony.

He begins, "Well, Your Honor, I am not familiar with your town here. My friend and I were heading out of town. You know, we went around that curve and were just about to the sign that says forty-five miles per hour. There is no way I could possibly have been going that fast. In fact, we had been following a real slow vehicle since the middle of town. I had looked at my speedometer as we went by the school, and we were doing about twenty-three miles per hour. I had been trying to get around that slow poke. And as we were about to get to a place where I could pass, the last car we met was the police car who was following a line of cars and was right behind a big old hay truck. As he went by us, I saw in my mirror that the cop turned real fast and came after us. I told my friend, 'This is going to be good. The cop is coming and is going to give this jerk ahead of us a ticket.' When the officer caught up to us, he turned on his lights. I pulled over to let him by and he pulled off behind me. I was shocked!

"When the officer came up to my window, I was upset and asked, 'Why did you stop behind me?' And that was when he told me I was speeding. I could not believe it. There is just no way possible that I was even going the speed limit, much less speeding."

I had been watching both the officer and Mr. Ordinary for body language and clues. A very curious and puzzled expression appears on the officer's face; he is flipping through his notebook reviewing his notes. The evidence is very different, including the location where the violation is alleged to have occurred.

The court, "Officer, do you have any questions for the witness?"

"Yes, Your Honor. Sir, isn't it true that I stopped you about one-quarter of a mile before the curve?"

"No, we were past the curve before we met you."

"I was stopped just past the school when you went by."

"No, we met you almost out of town."

"No further questions, Your Honor."

What I now have is an officer who seems confused and a defendant that seems certain about his facts. Very different stories, leaving a very big question in the court's mind.

"Are there any other witnesses or evidence?" asks the court.

"Yes, Your Honor," replies the defendant. "My friend can testify; he was with me and saw the whole thing."

The friend approaches, similar in appearance, a bit nervous, and is sworn in.

The court, "Sir, were you with Mr. Ordinary on the day the citation was issued?"

"Yes, sir."

"You were here in the courtroom and heard his testimony. Is your recollection of the facts different in any way from the testimony provided by Mr. Ordinary?"

"No, sir."

"Were you sitting in the passenger seat of the car?"

"Yes, sir. We were talking and looking around. Like Mr. Ordinary said, we were not familiar with this place. We had talking about things we saw and, like I said, we had never been here before and were just enjoying the drive. We had made several jokes about the slow car in front of us. When we saw the officer turned around we both were saying that the officer was going to get the other car."

"Is there anything else you would like to tell me about what you saw?"

"I don't think so. It was pretty much like Mr. Ordinary said."

At this point, the officer is now smiling, appears to be a bit eager to inquire of the witness.

"Officer, do you have any questions of this witness?"

"Yes, I do. Sir, where were you in the vehicle?"

"I was in the passenger seat."

"And the seat was one of those that goes all the way back and you were lying down at the time I stopped the vehicle, weren't you?"

"Yes, we had been driving a long ..." Hesitation in the

friend's voice, a cringe on the face of Mr. Ordinary, as the realization that the cat had just come out of the bag. "... time and I was really tired."

The officer continues, "When I approached the car you were asleep. You had been asleep, hadn't you?"

That exchange is followed by several, shall we call them, lame efforts to extricate one's self from the corner into which a friend has painted one. As Mr. Ordinary and his friend talk over each other, trying to explain how and why the rehearsed story has fallen apart, we wait. The more they talk, the worse it gets. Forty undertakers with crowbars could not pry the grin off of the officer's face.

So, let me get this right. While lying down and asleep, the friend observed all of the details to which the driver testified. Absent telepathic abilities or clairvoyant powers, we have arrived at that "point" wherein the weight of the evidence can now tilt the balance of the scales of justice. Then there is always the body language. Shaking heads, distorted faces, that figurative back peddling, if you know what I mean. Contrast that with the huge grin on the officer's face. Clunk. That is the sound of the scales of justice tilting emphatically against Mr. Ordinary.

An easy call for the court. Guilty as charged, and of course an appropriate fine. And, as a bonus, a stern lecture on perjury.

HONEST ... BUT ...

THE MAJORITY OF INDIVIDUALS WHO come before the court are ordinary, well-intentioned, honest, salt-of-the-earth kinds of people. Although a minor indiscretion may have provided them with the opportunity to appear before the court, they, for the most part, manage their lives in the ordinary course of human events consistent with rules and laws recognized by the majority of civilized society. These individuals operate within a realm of reason and common sense. This realm of reason and common sense is a relatively small area or playing field within which to act, interact, recreate, or work. Societal rules, norms, moral values, and laws imposed by legislators and courts keep the reasonable playing field somewhat limited in depth, breadth, height, and scope.

There are, however, quite a few individuals who are not limited or constrained by the boundaries of reasonableness or common sense. Though probably not the most scientific term, the most accurate term I can find for these people is that they are "special." Despite relative certainty of negative or adverse consequences, they will forge ahead in blind, linear-minded stubbornness, defying the laws of man, the laws of society, and sometimes even the laws of nature.

To summarize the prior two paragraphs, reason and common sense have a limited field within which to work. However, special people are not limited by direction or distance. The problem is that those individuals who reside most frequently outside the realm of reason occasionally pass through the field of reason and common sense and thus might momentarily be mistaken for ordinary and reasonable people.

A historical literary work has brought to my awareness the concept of identifying a particular class of individuals with an identifiable mark. A brand, as it were. To allow all those whom they met to know that they belonged to this special class. The scarlet letter was placed on the individual to represent to all that saw it a characteristic or quality regularly displayed by that individual.

All those individuals who decline to remain within the realm of reason, who decline the opportunity to play nice in the sandbox, who are willing to put you and all the people you love at risk should be required to wear a big, red "S" where it can be seen. That way, everyone who meets or sees them has a heads-up, a warning as it were, that this person is … "special." This designation would not be lightly considered and randomly awarded. Only when compelling evidence has mounted due to the individual's past performance should the big red "S" be applied. The big red "S" would have to be worn on the outer clothing or on a hat. Thus, at the first introduction, the viewer would know to be aware of the special propensity of the person.

This is a long-winded introduction for what will be a relatively short story. This is a description of an event that has unfolded before the court numerous times. At some point through the course of a court session, the name will be called. Mr. Notsosober will approach the bench. The Mr. Notsosobers tend to be early- to mid-range middle-aged men with a lengthy list of reasons why they are exempt from the normal requirements of society. They are generally un- or underemployed, and misapply their limited resources.

The citation will allege two or three, maybe even four violations. Two of which usually are the same. Those two will be driving while suspended and driving without insurance. The third or fourth citation may be anything from speeding to failure to obey a traffic-control device to failure to maintain a lane of travel.

Mr. Notsosober will always swagger or stagger forward to address the court and will be treating the situation either as beneath him, or as a humorous and entertaining matter. The conversation generally goes something like this:

"Mr. Notsosober, you are appearing here on three violations. The first is a speeding ticket for doing x number of miles per hour in an area posted something other than x. The other two citations are for driving while suspended and driving without insurance. How do you plead, Mr. Notsosober?"

"Well, I guess … I probably … Maybe uh … I guess I am probably guilty."

"Mr. Notsosober, did you know you were suspended before you drove?"

"Well, yes, I did know."

"Did you know you did not have insurance on your vehicle?"

"Yeah, I knew I did not have insurance also."

"Mr. Notsosober, can you tell me why you were driving?"

At this point, what the court is looking for is any reasonable explanation as to why someone with a suspended license and without insurance would be driving. One might expect a medical emergency, a stranded child, an aging parent in distress. However, the answer that follows is given with either a silly laugh or an air of righteous indignation.

"Well, the reason I was driving is, um, well, yeah, well, hmmm, we ran out of beer. Someone had to go get more beer. So I went."

At that point, there's generally an audible moan from the audience in the courtroom and the clerks and officers. Those present in the courtroom and experienced in court matters know that this excuse will not buy the defendant much sympathy. These Mr. Notsosobers generally have extensive driving records along with a history of failure to comply with societal rules and norms. Thus, the fine imposed is generally the same, the maximum fine on all counts.

No Good Deed
Should Go Unpunished

HARASSMENT. NOT A COMMON CITATION. Usually associated with a dysfunctional domestic situation. You know, the him and her, him with the new him and her, her with the new her and him, them with the neighbors, the want-to-be him for her or her for him or her … etc., etc.… ad nauseam. Generally, a sad story of an individual who cannot or will not just move on with his/her own life. So they bother, disturb, threaten, or in other words, harass the object of their disdain or affection. Makes one proud to be part of the evolutionarily advanced human species, does it not?

In one such case, the ticket had a large note stuck to the front that says, "Please read the report before court," and was signed by the officer. Unusual because the officers know that I will not read anything about the case before a guilty plea is entered or the defendant has been found guilty at trial. I follow this policy because I need to remain impartial and objective until all the evidence has been heard and a decision is made as to innocence or guilt. Despite the invitation in this case, I did not read the report or any information about the case.

The court calls the case, Mr. Goodman stands. He has been seated in the back row, doing his best to attempt to hide his presence in the courtroom. Tall young man, mid to late twenties, clean, well-groomed, with a muscular build, dark hair, good tan, probably works outdoors doing something manual. Quiet, soft countenance, moves easily for a large man, well coordinated and appears athletic. Appears embarrassed to be there. Eyes on the floor all the time he makes his way up to the front of the courtroom.

The court: "Mr. Goodman, you are appearing on a citation for harassment. How do you plead?"

A moment of silence, his eyes lift slowly to make eye contact with me and then with a pained expression and while shaking his head he says, "I guess I am guilty, Your Honor."

"Very well, if you can give me a moment to review the report." I then start reading the report that the officer had thought was so important. By the second paragraph of the report, it becomes obvious that this is a case that will require special handling out of the presence of the regular patrons of the court.

"Mr. Goodman, I will need to take this matter under advisement. You will need to have a seat and wait until the court has finished some other matters."

A look of concern replaces the embarrassed look, and Mr. Goodman compliantly takes a seat in the back of the courtroom. Court drags on and finally all other matters are done. Only Mr. Goodman remains.

"Mr. Goodman, please approach the bench and let me finish reading the report."

He moves swiftly to comply. I read the report. It reads as follows:

In response to a call from dispatch, I contacted Mr. Ohsohurt at the service station/convenience market. Mr. Ohsohurt stated that Mr. Goodman had shoved him, causing him to fall back and strike his back on a vehicle that was parked in front of the market. Mr. Ohsohurt refused medical treatment and insisted that Mr. Goodman be arrested and lodged in jail for assault and battery. Mr. Ohsohurt was very angry and shouted at me during the interview.

I then contacted Mr. Goodman in the market and asked that he accompany me to the parking lot to discuss the allegations made by Mr. Ohsohurt. As Mr. Goodman and I were proceeding through the parking lot, we were followed by several individuals who were volunteering and asking if they could make a statement also. I advised them I would take their statements as soon as I was done with Mr. Goodman. Mr. Goodman stated that he was waiting to pay for his gas in the market with many other people. There was only one clerk in the convenience market at that time. Mr. Ohsohurt became very angry about having to wait to pay for his purchases and began yelling at the clerk. The yelling included foul language and statements about the management and that they should have more clerks working. The profane yelling continued and then became personal and directed at the clerk. Mr. Goodman then stated that he approached Mr. Ohsohurt and asked him to stop cussing and yelling at the clerk, that she was doing the best she could. After several statements were exchanged, Mr. Ohsohurt invited Mr. Goodman out into the parking lot to "take care of this." Mr. Goodman agreed to go to the parking lot to get Mr. Ohsohurt out of the store. In the parking lot, Mr. Goodman stated that he stood there and listened to Mr. Ohsohurt for some time and Mr. Ohsohurt kept getting up real close to him, right in his face. Mr. Goodman told Mr. Ohsohurt to back off a little. When Mr. Ohsohurt did not, he put one hand in his chest and pushed him back. Mr. Ohsohurt (being smaller that Mr. Goodman) fell backwards and landed on a parked car. Mr. Ohsohurt got up and with more cussing told Mr. Goodman he was calling the police and that Mr. Goodman would go to jail for assaulting him. Mr. Ohsohurt then went to a phone and called 911.

I read several more pages of statements from the other witnesses and the clerk, all of whom had insisted on giving statements to the officer. The general consensus was that Mr. Ohsohurt had been, let me see, to quote, "rude, a jerk, nasty, an idiot," and paraphrasing some other comments, a rectum, the off-spring of a female dog, several speculations that he was born out of wedlock, and numerous comparisons to a piece of excrement and associated with being "loud mouthed." The final paragraph in the report read something like:

Mr. Ohsohurt insisted that Mr. Goodman be arrested and lodged. I refused to do that. I have written Mr. Goodman this citation to defuse the situation with Mr. Ohsohurt while at the convenience store and am relying on the court to handle this case appropriately. Attached to the report is Mr. Ohsohurt's criminal record. Mr. Goodman has no criminal record and no driving record."

I reviewed Mr. Ohsohurt's criminal record. Imagine that, several convictions for assault. Of course he knew what assault was: he had done it several times and done time for it. It is always a pleasure to see an expert in any field of work. As I looked up from reading the report, all three officers who were in the courtroom and both clerks were leaning forward, their eyes glaring hard to make eye contact with me. Though no word was spoken, they were screaming, "You had better get this one right!"

Now there is a dilemma here. Can society tolerate conduct deemed to be inappropriate when the circumstances under which it was provoked beg for a contrary conclusion? As the judge, can one condone or reward behavior that technically meets the criteria for a crime? The King Solomons and the great intellectual, legal, and judicial minds of the centuries may have a different opinion, but tonight, this is my courtroom. And, as an aside, there is no one on God's green earth that will appeal this decision! By now, Mr. Goodman is tense and quite nervous.

The court begins, "Mr. Goodman, please relax. How big a jerk was he?"

"Well, Your Honor, he was really rude and nasty to that clerk and he would not shut up. I know I should not have touched him, but he kept getting right up in my face. I am not trying to get out of anything, 'cause I did push him back a little. But it seemed to me that he fell back kind'a like intentionally a lot further that I pushed him. Kind'a like he was faking falling down. But I did push him."

"Did you know him at all before you saw him at the market?"

"No, sir, I don't believe I have ever seen him before."

"Then you would not have known that Mr. Ohsohurt has several convictions for assault?"

"No, I did not know that," a surprised look on his face.

"That is how he knew what to do when you pushed him. Mr. Goodman, this court does not believe that lecturing you on the rules of proper behavior or counseling you on the consequences of criminal conduct would serve any useful purpose. Thus, we will stipulate that I lectured you sternly on all those issues. You have entered a guilty plea, which the court will accept. You are hereby placed on probation for three days and, if there are no further incidents in that time period, this citation will be dismissed. To state it differently, three days from now, this citation will be dismissed and will never appear on your record. You were in a crowd of people, but you were the one who stepped up and helped out a person who needed it. You are to be commended. We need more people like you. You just need to be careful not to let an idiot get you into trouble. I apologize for making you wait until the end of court, but this was the forum I needed to dispose of the case in the way I felt it should be handled. You are free to leave. Have a great life."

Mr. Goodman smiled, approached the bench, and reached out his large callused hand, which I was proud to shake. The officers and clerks relaxed, court was over and they would not have to beat me to within an inch of my life on this evening.

Yes, I Am That Bullheaded

PERSONALITY TRAITS AND HUMAN CHARACTERISTICS do not always have the consistency or predictability of mathematical equations. However, there are a couple of traits that uniformly and almost without exception seem to be companions. This particular companionship provides a limited mathematical predictability. So consistent are these companions that the two characteristics can be reversed in the mathematical equation and yet the balance and value of the equation remain unchanged.

Those two characteristics are ignorance and arrogance. Thus, the ignorance of arrogance or the arrogance of ignorance. Symmetry at perhaps its lowest level. They also seem to have a Siamese twin-like quality. When either element is found in the gray matter located between the ears of an individual, the companion twin is nearby. There are those who choose to stand on the platform of ignorance or arrogance. Why? That is one of many questions to which I do not have the answer.

This next young man somehow seemed committed to being an outstanding example of the above-proffered thesis.

The docket of new citations is arranged in alphabetical order. Citations are taken at the beginning of the court primarily from tradition, but also to provide the "one-and-only's" an opportunity to appear, deal with the court, and get on with their otherwise law-abiding lives. Those who are regular attendees need the opportunity to continue to experience more courtroom time to encourage them to deviate from their chosen ill-fated path. The hope is that they will then embark, launch, redirect, or start on a new path in life.

Working through the docket on this particular evening, we arrived at the name of a person that hereinafter will be known as Mr. Hitme. When his name was called, he was standing near the back of the courtroom by the door. As he began moving toward the front of the room, he was somewhat rude as he nudged or pushed people and bulldozed his way to the front of the courtroom. He stood with hands on hips, one foot slightly in front of the other, and head and neck protruding up and forward. Hard eyes, very hard eyes. He was tall, six feet one or six feet two, muscular build, pointed face. Somewhat similar to Ichabod Crane in appearance. Greasy, dark, medium-length hair. Jeans probably two sizes too small and thus very tight. So tight that perhaps the jeans were contributing to what appeared to be his overall discomfort with or anger at life in general.

The court begins, "Mr. Hitme, you are appearing on ... now, let me see, one, two, three different citations. No, four, five, that would be six citations. That is interesting. Now let's see, two citations issued on one date, approximately forty minutes apart. The next pair of citations was issued the very next day, about two hours apart. Then the third pair of citations was issued two days later, once again about two hours apart. Let's take them one at a time, chronologically, starting with the first citation.

"Mr. Hitme, you are appearing on citations for speeding, driving while suspended, and no insurance. How do you plead?"

"Guilty," blurts out Mr. Hitme, with some degree of pride. At this point, the court is going to give Mr. Hitme an opportunity to explain the situation. What the court is looking for is any reasonable or rational basis for Mr. Hitme to have been driving without a license and without insurance.

"Would you like to tell me what was going on? Why you were driving without a license, and without insurance?"

"I have to go to work," he almost yelled.

"So, you knew you were suspended and you drove anyway?"

"Yeah, well, I have gotta go to work. The only way I have to go to work is to drive."

"OK. Let me review your driving record. I see by your driving record this is not the first time you have dealt with traffic citations, Mr. Hitme. However, I will impose minimum fines on all three counts. Let's move on to the next citation. About forty-five minutes later, you were cited by the same police officer for driving while suspended and no insurance. How do you plead on those citations?"

"I'm guilty on those, too." Once again real defiance, real arrogance. The depth, breadth, and scope of Mr. Hitme's miscalculation is now about to blossom into full bloom.

"So, let me get this straight, Mr. Hitme. You received a citation for driving while suspended and with no insurance.

The officer cuts you some slack and lets you drive your truck home. And then within forty-five minutes you are out and driving again, and drive right back in front of the same officer?"

"Well, like I told you, I've gotta drive. I've gotta go to work. I've gotta do the things I've gotta do. And I am going to drive to get those done."

"So, even if you know you are violating the law, and by not having insurance you are exposing all the rest of us to the consequences of your indiscretion, you are going to drive because you think you have to, to go to work?"

"Well, yeah, I've gotta go to work. That is the only way I can get any money to pay my bills."

"Well, Mr. Hitme, you need to comply with the traffic rules and regulations just like everybody else. Due to your intentional conduct, I will impose the maximum fines on these two citations."

Here we are. The moment of truth. Will Mr. Hitme accept my decision, or will the fool now be willingly brought out, polished up, and presented to the world for all to see? He launches into it: "That's a bunch of crap. I have gotta go to work, and the only way I can get to work is to drive and you are going to hit me with a big fine like that? That is just a bunch of s—t. I am not going to take this crap. Not only that, I am going to keep on driving 'cause, like I keep telling you, I gotta go to work and I've gotta drive to get there."

"Very well, Mr. Hitme, let's move on to the next ticket that was issued the next morning. How do you plead on that, driving while suspended and with no insurance?"

"I plead guilty. You can hit me again. You can hit me with all the fines you want. I am not going to pay them anyway."

"Very well, I will impose maximum fines on those citations. And now, move on to the third citation …"

Mr. Hitme interrupts, "I'll just plead guilty on all of them and you can hit me with that maximum fine as much as you want; it is not going to change what I am going to do."

"OK then, on the remaining four citations I will accept guilty pleas on all eight counts. I will impose maximum fines on each of those eight counts. Mr. Hitme, I am going to set your payments at $100 a month. First payment will be due thirty days from today. If you do not make that payment, you will need to be back in court on that date to advise me as to what your status is. If you do not make a payment and you do not make an appearance, a warrant will be issued for your arrest. Upon your arrest you will be lodged in the county jail, do you understand that?"

"Yeah, I hear what you are saying, but I don't understand and I am not going to pay your fines. That is a whole lot of money. I'd have to work a lot of months to pay off all those."

"Mr. Hitme, you will need to be quiet and keep your mouth shut in the courtroom for the rest of your time here today. As I advised you, if you do not make payments as scheduled, I will issue a warrant for your arrest. However, the amount of your fines is substantial. That is one point we will agree on. I will give you an opportunity to work your way out of this. If you stop driving until you get a license and insurance, and you show me a good payment history of $100 a month for a period of time, I will consider dismissing the majority of the fines I have imposed today. However, you need to understand that each and every time you appear before me on a driving-while-suspended or no-insurance citation, I will impose maximum fines. Do you understand that? If you do, just nod your head yes." Whereupon Mr. Hitme glares at the bench, shakes his head indignantly, and folds his arms across his chest.

"Very well, Mr. Hitme, you are done here today. You are to leave the courtroom right now."

Whereupon Mr. Hitme does an about-face and blows through the crowd like a bowling ball through bowling pins as he exits the courtroom.

As we were reviewing the events of the evening at the close of the court session that day, we dubbed this gentleman Mr. Hitme. To this day, he still holds the record for the most fines and the biggest total fines imposed at a single court session.

*   *   *

Two weeks later, Mr. Hitme is back in court again on another citation: driving while suspended, no insurance. A repeat of the previous performances is endured, guilty pleas accepted, maximum fines imposed.

Approximately two weeks later, when first payment is due, Mr. Hitme appears in court. In due course, his name is called.

"Mr. Hitme, you're appearing in court tonight, I am assuming, in lieu of payment."

"Well, I was really mad and upset last time after court so I did not go to work. I got fired from my job so I can't afford to make your payment. I am trying to find a new job right now."

"Very well, Mr. Hitme. You will be appearing in this court

three times a month until you are able to start making your payments. I would remind you and advise you not to drive anymore."

At about this point, I notice a woman in the back of the courtroom who stands, interrupts the court, and asks to be heard. The conversation goes something like this. It begins with the court.

"Ma'am, who are you?"

"I am Mr. Hitme's mother."

"Very well, ma'am, if you would like to approach the bench, I will listen briefly to something you have to say, so long as it is relevant to the matter before the court."

While Mother Hitme is moving toward the front of the courtroom, I notice a strong family resemblance. Not necessarily in physical appearance, but in the scowl on the face, the mean look in the eyes, and the generally nasty attitude. She approached the bench and she begins.

"When my son came home a few weeks ago and told me what had happened, I could not believe it. I cannot imagine that you expect him to pay that kind of a fine."

"Ma'am, the court's disposition of the matter of your son's traffic tickets is a matter between your son and this court. I will explain to you what I explained to your son and that is that if he begins obeying the law and not driving until he gets his license and insurance and shows me a good payment history, I will dismiss a substantial amount of the fine. However, he is going to have to comply with those requirements before I will even consider that. Now, do you have anything else to say that might have any bearing on the matter that is currently before the court?"

"Well, I just don't think that it's fair—" and the court interrupts.

"Ma'am, quite frankly your opinion of what is fair is irrelevant. I have imposed penalties on the citations that were before me, and I am going to stand by those with the conditions I have placed on them. Mr. Hitme, you will need to appear in court two weeks from right now unless you get a payment made by then. That will be all."

Over the following several months, Mr. Hitme appeared in every court as scheduled. What began as a nasty attitude evolved into intense dislike, toward me personally and life in general. After several months of appearances, Mr. Hitme's arrogance took over, and he just stopped coming to court as scheduled, whereupon a warrant was issued. Mr. Hitme was lodged in jail several times over the next many months, but no fine payments were made.

Then what we always hope for happened. The court session began. Seated in the back of the courtroom was Mr. Hitme with a different aura about him. A different attitude visibly displayed. Head bowed and a milder countenance. He was not on the docket; however, there was an outstanding warrant for his arrest.

After the court finishes the docket and all the other matters have been handled, the court turns its attention to Mr. Hitme.

"Mr. Hitme, please approach the bench." Whereupon Mr. Hitme, followed by a middle-aged gentleman, approached the bench. The gentleman accompanying Mr. Hitme begins.

"Your Honor, I am here with Mr. Hitme today to ask the court to show a little leniency and let me work with Mr. Hitme and see if we can provide him with an opportunity to work his way out of this situation."

"Sir, I am certainly willing to listen to anything reasonable in that regard."

"I am an owner of a business in a neighboring small town. I became aware of Mr. Hitme through a friend of mine who asked if I could give him a job. I have talked with him at length and have given him an opportunity to come work for me. However, I need to be sure that he will be at work and that he will not be lodged in jail for not paying fines to the court. So, what I am proposing to the court is if you will pull the warrant so that he can come to work, I have talked with Mr. Hitme and he has agreed to allow me to deduct from his paycheck each month an amount he can afford to pay on the fines. I will mail that directly into the court."

"Sir, that is a most generous opportunity you have given to Mr. Hitme. Just out of curiosity, are you a relative or an acquaintance of his?"

"No, sir. I would just like to give the kid a chance to see if he can find a way to turn his life around and get on the right track."

"Mr. Hitme, you have been standing there listening to everything that has been said. If I pull the warrant, are you willing to have this gentleman deduct from your paycheck enough to make payments to the court while you are working for him?"

A quieter, kinder Mr. Hitme nods vigorously and says, "Yes, Your Honor, I have agreed to that. I need to have a chance to turn my life around and see if I can get myself straightened out."

"Very well. Court will agree to what has been proposed. I will schedule the first payment for thirty days from now. That should give you an opportunity to go through at least two pay cycles to accumulate the payment. Mr. Hitme, let me remind you of the offer I made you. You make your payments on time and don't get any more tickets for a period of time, and I will be open to discussing dismissal of all warrant fees and some of the fines. Now, sir (addressing the gentleman who is with Mr. Hitme), I am going to impose an additional condition on you, and that is that if Mr. Hitme does not appear for work as scheduled, or you terminate his employment, I would ask you to advise the court immediately so we can schedule his next appearance and issue warrants if he does not appear."

"That is fine with me, sir. I would be glad to do that. Can I get an address of where to send the payments?"

"You bet. The clerk here will give you the address and the phone number so you can have those available to you. Mr. Hitme, I hope you know what a unique opportunity you have here. I hope you take advantage of this opportunity."

The gentleman responds, "Oh, I think he will, Your Honor. I think we can work together, and Mr. Hitme will find out how much better life can be if he takes care of business. Thank you for the time and consideration."

At which time, Mr. Hitme and his newfound best friend exit the court.

Thirty days went by. The first payment arrived. Another thirty days went by. The second payment arrived. Two weeks went by. The clerk of the court received a phone call from the gentleman who had given Mr. Hitme the job. He advised the court that Mr. Hitme's conduct on the job could not be tolerated and that he had been terminated. A letter was sent to Mr. Hitme advising him of his next court date. Of course, he did not appear and a warrant was issued. Once again, over the following months, a series of warrants were issued. On each new warrant, Mr. Hitme was lodged, released, and ordered to appear at court and then would disappear again for a period of months.

A new day, new events in the life of Mr. Hitme. The court receives a notice of a filing of bankruptcy. Soon thereafter, Mr. Hitme appears in court and advises the court that his lawyer informs him that his bankruptcy has reduced the fines and that he will be making payments into the bankruptcy court. Mr. Hitme is advised that so long as he makes his payments to bankruptcy court, the bankruptcy court will forward the appropriate payment to the city.

A few weeks later, a 911 call was received at the police department. An ambulance and police officers were dispatched to Mr. Hitme's residence. Mr. Hitme was rushed to the hospital, narrowly clinging to life, following an apparent suicide attempt by a drug overdose. Inquiries at the hospital the following day indicated that Mr. Hitme had not been successful in the suicide attempt and had survived. Following Mr. Hitme's recovery from the suicide attempt, the court received notice of dismissal from bankruptcy for failure to make payments as scheduled. Thereafter, Mr. Hitme was back suffering the consequences of his choices and wallowing in the ignorance of his arrogance. It is hard to quantify the magnitude of this tragedy. The loss of opportunity, the waste of effort, energy, talents, and intellect by this young man to this point in his life is sad.

But despair not—the following story addresses the other side of the same coin. In this next story, the ignorance of arrogance, or the arrogance of ignorance, was left behind as history, an opportunity was accepted, and a life was rebuilt and renewed with opportunity.

Occasionally, a Phoenix Does Rise

Turning over the new leaf, starting over, renewed commitment. Frequently promised, seldom delivered. Miraculous when it appears. Moment-marking and spectacular when witnessed. I have no illusion that I sit at the focal point, the hinge as it were, on which turns or swings the change in an individual's life. Rather, the court sits in the unenviable position of creating a negative consequence for deviation from societal norms, rules, or laws. Most people tend to follow the path of least resistance. Thus, as negative consequences build, eventually most people will redirect their efforts and energy and follow the less problematic, more pleasant, pleasurable, and rewarding paths. Although we as humans claim to be advanced as a species, we are not all on the same rung in our march up the evolutionary ladder. Individually we have different learning capacities coupled with different levels of willingness to change or alter our behavior.

The vast majority of people who come through the muni-court system are good folks who have woopsed. The other small percentage of court patrons are those who do not think the rules apply to them. They are misled by their pride, arrogance, addiction, and several other derailing personal choices and habits. It is the burden of those of us who work in the system to be observers and bystanders as these people self-destruct before our eyes. Occasionally, from within this parade of human carnage and wasted lives that pass in through the court system, that single solitary individual rises above the average and beats the odds. This is one such story.

He was in his late teens when he first appeared in court. A little taller than average, unkempt, dressed in what one would call sloppy dress. However, it seemed to be the style of the time. He had an indifferent attitude regarding his appearances in court. He was visibly blatant and openly indifferent toward fines imposed or advice offered. He appeared in front of the court on several different occasions on different combinations of citations. There were several for driving while suspended. On each of those occasions, maximum fines had been imposed.

On more than one occasion, he had been lodged in jail on a warrant for failure to appear or for failure to make payments as the court had ordered. Once again, his demonstrable indifference to the experience of going to jail would seem to have put this young man on the road to joining the nonconformist crowd, the confused, the geniuses at self-destruction, those stubbornly committed to nonconforming, self-destructive, antisocial behavior.

Frequently, individuals who are scheduled to appear before the court are lodged in the county jail for other misconduct. A police officer is dispatched to retrieve the individuals, who are then brought to court. They will appear in prison dress, which is green, medical scrublike slipover shirt and pants, white socks, and rubber slip-on sandals. To complete the sartorial splendor, the always popular and never favorite customized jewelry provided exclusively by the county jail: handcuffs for some individuals and, for the occasional "special person," leg shackles as well. The court handles these individuals first so they can be returned to the county jail at the earliest possible moment.

The conversation on this particular night goes something like this:

"Mr. Phoenix, you are appearing from the county jail tonight?"

He rises, appearing to be uncomfortable as he approaches the bench. This is new. I notice a difference in his overall attitude. The indifferent cavalier attitude is not present. With a more somber tone he says, "Yes, Your Honor."

"Mr. Phoenix, I am assuming you are doing time in the county jail on something other than a warrant from this court."

"Yes, Your Honor."

"How long are you going to be in jail?"

"Your Honor, I'm doing thirty days, but I probably will get out in about fourteen to sixteen days."

"Very well. I will sign a release order on a warrant from this court. I am writing on the warrant that upon your release from the county jail, you are to call this courthouse. Find out when the next court date is and appear in court at that time. Do you understand this?"

"Yes, Your Honor, but could I ask you something?"

"Certainly, go ahead."

"Your Honor, I have reached a point in my life where I have had to admit that I am a junkie. I have the chance to get into an institutional facility to help me but it is not in this county. If I get into the program, I will not be able to appear in court, and since I won't have a job, I won't be able to make payments. If you issue a warrant for me, they will kick me out of the program and I do not think that will help me much either. I want to know if there is some way we can work this out."

"Mr. Phoenix, I am pleased to hear that you are entering a program and yes, there is a way we can work this out. What I will need from you is written confirmation from the program in which you are enrolled. The letter will need to state that it is an institutional, in-house program. I need to know how long you will be there, and I will need a commitment from the program that if you walk away from the program, or get kicked out of the program, that they will advise the court immediately. If I get that written confirmation from you, then I will suspend your next appearance and your payments until you complete the program. However, when you complete the program, you are going to have to come back to court and let me know what your plans are and how we are going to resolve your obligation to the city. Do you understand that?"

"Yes, Your Honor. Thank you. I don't think that will be a problem."

Two weeks go by. I generally try to arrive about a half an hour before court to take care of administrative matters. This night, included in the documents for review is a letter from a rehabilitation facility in a neighboring county that advises that Mr. Phoenix is an inpatient there and will remain there for approximately six months. The letter also advises that they will notify the court if Mr. Phoenix walks off or is terminated from the program. With that information, we docket Mr. Phoenix's next appearance out for about six and a half months.

About six months go by. In court on that night, we get to the end of the docket. There is one young man left sitting in the back row of the courtroom. It is common to have people not on the docket appear with questions or with other issues they want to discuss with the court. As a matter of courtesy, I inquire as to their purpose in court.

"Sir, are you a spectator, a visitor of the court, or is there something we can help you with this evening?"

The young man stands. Kind of smiles at first and then his face breaks out into a full grin as he approaches the bench. He begins, "You don't recognize me, do you?"

"No, sir, I do not believe I do."

With a smile that is about to explode off his face, he says, "My name is Mr. Phoenix."

Shock obviously registers on my face. I look down the bench at the clerk and the officers of the court. Their faces reflect an equally shocked or surprised expression. None of us even recognized him.

"That is a good thing," he says. "I just got released from the program, which I successfully completed. But I am here to ask the court for another favor."

"Go ahead; I can hardly wait to hear what you have to say. I am surprised at your appearance. I must confess I did not recognize you at all."

"Your Honor, I have successfully completed the program.

However, I have a chance to get into a vocational training program up in the northern part of the state. It is a six-month-long program, where I can get follow-up help with my drug addictions. I can continue to have some behavior modification and anger management support work and I can get vocational training. I will not be earning any money while I am there. If I am enrolled in the northern part of the state, I will not have the ability to come to court. I am guessing that if you agree to this, then the same conditions will apply that you put on me when I went to the drug treatment facility. My counselor has told me that they will be glad to give you a letter confirming that I am in the program and telling you how long I will be in the program. Right now, I am expected to be in there four to six months."

"Mr. Phoenix, congratulations. It is rare that we see success stories like yours even at the in-house drug treatment facilities. The court would be glad to extend your next appearance for an additional six months or for so long as you are enrolled in the program. Will you have that information to us before the next court date, which is in two weeks?"

"Yes, Your Honor, I will have that to you. I just want to make sure I have the correct address and fax number so I can get that sent to you."

After verifying the address and fax numbers, he politely excuses himself and leaves the courtroom.

By the next time we appear at court, there is a new letter from Mr. Phoenix's counselor. The letter states that he is enrolled in the vocational training program, where he will be for approximately six months. His counselor also confirms that if he walks away from the program, or is involuntarily discharged from the program, the court will be notified. Mr. Phoenix's next appearance is docketed out for another six months.

Before the six months lapses, another letter arrives from the vocational school. Mr. Phoenix's counselors ask for an extension of time for Mr. Phoenix to complete additional vocational training. The counselor confirms that he is meeting all expectations and performing and participating on an acceptable level.

Some five and a half to six months later, as the courtroom is clearing out, I notice Mr. Phoenix is sitting in the back. This time I recognized him. Clean-cut, well dressed, bright eyes, smile on his face, indifferent only to his surroundings, waiting in anticipation for his turn to address the court. I call his name first while there is still a crowd in the courtroom.

"Mr. Phoenix, would you like to approach the bench?"

He arises briskly. "Yes, Your Honor."

He moves swiftly to the front of the courtroom carrying a folder with several documents, neatly arranged, paper-clipped together, and tucked under his arm. As he approaches, he looks me directly in the eye and says, "Good evening, Your Honor."

"Good evening, Mr. Phoenix, it is good to see you again. How are you doing?"

"Great! I am appearing in the court tonight to give you an update on my progress. I would like to begin by thanking the court for working with me as I have been through the various programs. I would like to take a moment and show you what I have done."

"Mr. Phoenix, it appears that you have documents you

would like the court to review. Please hand them to the officer who will then pass them up to me."

"Your Honor, the first thing I'd like to show you is my certificate of completion for the drug treatment facility. You will see that I completed that a little over a year ago. Next are my certificates of accomplishment that I have received while I have been in the vocational training."

He hands a stack of documents to the officer who passes them up to the bench. I review the documents. They are certificates of completion in courses in carpentry, plumbing, electrical wiring, leadership, and numerous other citations of accomplishment and commendations for exemplary behavior. There are also several letters from counselors, instructors, and administrators from the vocational training facility extolling the exceptional attitude, work ethic, and accomplishments of this young man.

Moments like these are very few in our court. So many of the individuals who have been habitual offenders never seem to turn the corner and move their lives past the revolving door going nowhere. However, this is a glorious example that such change is possible.

"Mr. Phoenix, you are to be commended. This is truly incredible. You certainly have made the most of these opportunities. What are your plans now?"

"Your Honor, I need to ask one more favor from you. I do not have a job yet. I am looking for a job, and I will have one soon. I have financial obligations I need to pay back for my schooling, and I need to become financially independent to support myself. So … I need a little bit of time before I can start making payments, and when I do, if you can make them really small until I can get myself up and going again, I promise I will pay off everything I owe for the fines."

"Mr. Phoenix, we can do better than that. We will make your first payment due in ninety days. If you have not found a job or are not able to make a payment in ninety days, come back to court and we will work with you until you can get your payments started. We can set payments at $25 a month if that's an acceptable figure."

"Yes, sir, that would be fine."

"Not only that, Mr. Phoenix, if you show me a good payment history and stay out of trouble, the court will dismiss all of your warrant fees and a substantial amount of your fines. As you are well aware, on several of your citations I imposed maximum penalties. The purpose of the maximum penalties is to get your attention and create a negative consequence sufficient enough to cause you to comply with the vehicle code that you insisted on violating. The court has the ability to and will dismiss a significant amount of those fines and the warrant fees that you have accumulated so long as you convince the court that you have, in fact, turned over a new leaf."

He smiled, his eyes twinkled, "Well, Your Honor, get ready to dismiss some fines."

"Mr. Phoenix, it will be my pleasure."

He departed that evening and that is the last time I ever saw him. A few weeks later, payments of $25 a month began appearing. A few months after that, the payments increased voluntarily. A few months after that, the payments were substantial and had been sustained, and a year had gone by. The majority of the total fine and warrant fees were thereafter dismissed. Mr. Phoenix was sent a letter advising him that he had fulfilled his obligation to the city and that no further payment need be made.

It is an incredible experience to watch a metamorphosis—indifference and despair rolling into a cocoon and emerging positive, enthusiastic, and prepared to soar. It is one of life's true joys. From time to time, the memory of this young man floats through my consciousness and, every time it does, there is a momentary warm glow as I think of the good things I expect are happening in this person's life.

JUST A GOOD
OLE COUNTRY KID

O N A WARM SUMMER DAY, early in the afternoon, the chief of police stood in the entryway of City Hall. Hands slightly above his hips, resting on the police belt on which the usual array of stuff was hung, slung, hooked, or clipped. As the chief surveyed Main Street through the glass windows of the door, he spotted it: a crime in progress. Directly across the street from City Hall, all alone, an old pickup truck was parked snuggly next to the curb facing the wrong direction. Ooh. You could see the direction of the traffic flow on that side of the street was from the Chief's right to left. The pickup truck was clearly and unmistakably facing left to right. Therefore, a clear violation of the law. Yes, you may have guessed this one, illegal parking.

A reserve officer was dispatched across the street to locate the driver of the pickup, have the pickup moved, and ticket the driver. The anxious reserve officer, under constant surveillance by the chief, checked several businesses and was unable to locate the driver. After returning to run the plates through the Department of Motor Vehicles to determine who the registered owner was, the officer elected to fill out a ticket and leave it on the windshield for the registered owner. Task accomplished. Duty fulfilled.

Evening court session, several weeks later. The court calls the name on the ticket for illegal parking.

"Mr. Hick," calls the court.

In the back of the courtroom, a young man, seventeen to eighteen, stands and timidly makes his way to the front of the court. The young man sports a home-given haircut, which had been covered by a baseball hat that he held in his hand. Wearing very worn cowboy boots that were several sizes too big, worn jeans, and a shirt, everything old but clean. The young man looks very much out of place. His eyes blink frequently. He is obviously very worried and concerned.

"Mr. Hick?" asks the court.

"No, sir, Your Honor," answers the young man in a polite, deep country drawl. "I'm his son."

The court asks, "May I ask why you are appearing instead of Mr. Hick?"

"Well, sir, ya see, I was driving the truck the day it got the ticket put on it. My dad was not too happy to find out that he got a ticket while I was driving his truck, so he sent me to straighten everythang out."

"The court thanks you for your honesty, sir, but we will have to reissue the ticket in your name. You understand that this is a citation for illegal parking?"

"Yes, sir, I do now. But honest, sir, I did not know that then when I parked that way."

"Before we reissue the ticket, why don't you tell me why you parked the wrong way on the street?"

The young man looks down at the floor, shakes his head several times, inhales, exhales, inhales, looks up at the court, extends both arms out from his shoulders in full span and, with a furred brow and a sincere look on his face, says, "Well, sir, I'm just a country hick. We live on a ranch thirteen miles off the paved road. While it might not be just right, I have been driving for many years on the ranch, but I don't drive much here in town. Out there, sir, on the ranch, nobody cares how you park so long as you are out of the way. I did not know you wasn't suppose to park thataway. I know that now and you can be sure that I will never do that again. I just saw a friend of mine on the sidewalk. There was no one coming, so I pulled over to talk to him. I got out and we walked down to the store to get a Coke. When I come back, there was that ticket on the windshield. The only thing I can tell you is that I am just a country hick that didn't know no better. But you can bet I will never do that again in your town."

Touched by the young man's innocence and sincerity, the court struggles to maintain judicial composure while fighting the urge to either laugh or give him a hug. In the world of high crimes and criminals, this one just is not.

The court, "You do understand now that you are required to park with your pickup pointed in the same direction as the flow of traffic?"

"Yes, sir, I do now."

"With your assurance that you will not do it again, sir, I will dismiss this ticket for your father and you this time. Please tell your father that the ticket in his name will be dismissed. Thank you for coming in."

A moment passed while the result settled in the young

man's mind. A look of relief slowly replaced the look of fear and concern on his face. He quietly and politely thanked the court, turned, and, as though inclined to run, visibly forced himself to walk deliberately but slowly out of the court. Then, placing his hat on just as he exited the door, he broke into a full run disappearing into the parking lot.

Never Judge a Book ...

SPEEDING TICKETS. ONE OF THE best sellers at this court. Lots of "one-and-only's" make their only foray into the world of municipal court after an indiscretion involving speed (velocity of motor vehicles, not the drug). Local police officers know that this court is not likely to give serious consideration to any citation for speeds under ten miles over the posted speed limit unless there are special circumstances like speeding in a school zone. Thus, as speeding tickets come up on the docket, what I expect to see is something like eleven to twenty miles over the posted limit for first- and only-time offenders.

People appearing on speeding tickets usually deny having gone as fast as the citation states, but admit to speeding. As fines go, speeding is not as expensive as other things. So, the "one-and-only's" generally, while not thrilled about being there, take their shot at trying to get off with a heartfelt explanation and a promise never to do it again. Then with some degree of decorum and civility, they pay their fine and disappear back into the anonymity of the conforming masses. Occasionally, someone will make a comment about a small town speed trap or this "podunk town." Although we have no zoo in town and are north of the equator, something about a kangaroo is occasionally mentioned in association with the court, though this is generally after a trial.

There are two types of speeding tickets: first, exceeding the posted speed limit (this one is pretty obvious), and second, violation of the "basic rule." The "basic rule" is that you should go no faster that the conditions existing at the time reasonably allow. Makes sense, right? If the road is wet, icy, or foggy, there is white stuff on it, or children are running in the street, you do not get to go the posted limit and do damage to yourself, others, or (depending on the child) to children.

A key point to remember for the rest of this chapter is never, ever, ever judge a book by the quiet, refined, sophisticated, educated look of the cover.

The court: "Ms. Composed."

She is forty to forty-five, tall, and slender. Well-groomed and tastefully dressed. Soft-spoken, articulate, with a sense of purpose. Almost distinguished. She is polite to the other people in the row as she works her way to the aisle. Several "excuse me's," taking great care not to step on anyone's feet. She approaches the bench and says, "Yes, Your Honor."

"Ma'am, you are appearing on a speeding ticket, doing," I then look at the alleged speed, "seventy-four in a posted forty-five zone. How do you plead?"

"Not guilty."

"Trial will be set in two weeks. You will need to return at that time. Bring any witnesses or evidence you would like the court to consider. Do you have any questions?"

"No, thank you, Your Honor," says she and then departs.

Two weeks pass, the court is in session. We have reached

the point in the proceeding where the trials will be held. In muni court there is no jury, just me.

"Ms. Composed," calls the court.

She stands up in the back and with grace and efficiency takes her place in front of the bench next to the officer.

"Officer, is the city ready to proceed?"

"Yes, Your Honor." The officer is sworn in and proceeds like a broken record. "On blankety-blank date, at one thirty-five in the morning (just after midnight) I was on duty as an officer for the city. I was in a marked patrol car, in uniform, badge prominently displayed. I was heading north on the highway just south of the "S" curves when I saw a vehicle approaching at a high rate of speed. I activated my radar and clocked the speed of the oncoming car at seventy-four miles per hour. I am trained in the operation of radar and the radar had been tested prior to my shift and at the end of my shift that day and was found to be functioning properly. The posted speed limit in that location is forty-five miles per hour. As the vehicle went past me, I turned around and activated the lights and siren. As I caught up with the vehicle, the vehicle pulled over to the shoulder. I approached the vehicle, identified the driver as Ms. Composed by her driver's license, and issued her a citation for violation of the basic rule for doing seventy-four in the curves in a zone posted at forty-five miles per hour." He says it all without ever inhaling.

"Ma'am, do you have any questions of the officer, as in cross-examination?" inquires the court.

"No, Your Honor," responds Ms. Composed.

Ms. Composed is then placed under oath and invited to present her case to the court.

"Ma'am, what would you like to tell me?"

"It was about one thirty in the morning. The officer and I were the only two cars on the road. I had been driving for a long time and was in a hurry to get home. I am an excellent driver. You can check my driving record. (With that invitation, I looked at her driving record and there were no other citations listed.) I was almost out of the city limits."

She continues, "I was cited for violation of the basic rule. The road was dry. The sky was clear. The moon was near full. I had good visibility, and my vehicle is capable of taking those curves at a much higher speed and I had slowed down for the curves. I researched the law and was driving reasonably for the conditions at the time. Therefore, I am not guilty, and the ticket should be dismissed."

"How fast were you going?"

"I'm not sure."

"Do you dispute the officer's statement that you were going seventy-four?"

"No, sir."

"Well then, based on the evidence, I find you guilty and will impose the statutory minimum fine for that speed. Can you pay the fine tonight?"

At this point Ms. Composed changes or decomposes into Ms. "I'm-irritated-with-you."

Now with a fair amount of attitude, she responds. "I am not going to pay the fine because this is not right," she blurts out. A decided change with a continued degradation in attitude. Ms. Composed is decomposing into Ms. Truecolors.

"Ma'am, I understand you may not agree with my decision. But if you do not pay the fine, the court will resort to other alternatives to encourage your compliance. Or you can appeal my decision to the county court."

"I want you to explain this to me."

"Very well. It is the opinion of this court that seventy-four miles an hour in town and on those curves is unreasonable and dangerous."

"If it was dangerous, why did I not have a wreck?"

"Ma'am, I am not going to debate this with you. I will give you thirty days to pay the fine or be back in court to explain why you have not paid it."

At which time, Ms. Composed exits, not by leaving the building but by giving way to a new personality. Ms. "Righteously Indignant" enters. Arms now fold across chest. Voice louder and almost openly defiant.

"I am going to stay right here until you can explain this to me," she states.

"Well, ma'am, I have explained."

"You have not," she interrupts.

At this point, Ms. Righteously Indignant metamorphoses before my very eyes into a new creature that can best be described as the "I am the unstoppable force." I counter by assuming the mantel of the "unmovable object." Anger has a constant companion, a Siamese twin as it were, and that is stupidity. The unstoppable force being steered by stupidity races to the collision with the unmovable object.

"Ma'am, if you do not move aside so I can continue on with the next case, I will have the officers remove you from the courtroom."

"I am staying right here until you get this thing right," she replies defiantly.

"This is the last time I am going to ask you to move aside. Will you move aside?"

"Absolutely not!"

"Officers, take her into custody and remove her from the courtroom."

Whereupon three officers step forward and handcuff Ms. Composed and physically take her to the back of the courtroom. It has become the custom of this court to hold those who need to be restrained until the end of the court session and allow them a chance to cool off and de-Siamese from stupidity. Then I do the "do we have your attention now?" or the "do you really want to go to jail?" speech. One would expect to hear yada, yada, apology accepted and life goes on. However, as the court is proceeding with the next case, I can hear Ms. Composed's voice in the back of the court. She is not happy. Although I cannot discern exactly what is being said, it is likely that the possibility of the officers' or my canine ancestry and speculation that my parents were not married at the time of my birth is being discussed. Shortly thereafter, the door opens and the officers and Ms. Composed exit.

A couple of cases later, the chief of police approaches the bench. I finish the pending case and direct my attention to the chief.

"Your Honor," begins the chief, "Ms. Composed would not be quiet, so we took her outside. She would not cooperate, so we put her in the police car.

She is now trying to kick the windows out. I would request permission to lodge her in the county jail."

"By all means, Chief, and if she does any damage to the

patrol car, add destruction of city property to the contempt of court charge."

Ms. Composed goes to jail. Ms. Composed gets the full experience. Jailhouse photo, fingerprints, full body search, and the always-popular jail greens to wear. Sartorial splendor well beneath anything Ms. Composed owns or is accustomed to wearing. The "unstoppable force" is, after all, apparently stoppable.

A few days pass. Quite peacefully, I might add. Then, a call from the court clerk. It seems that Ms. Composed has retained an attorney. A deal is being offered. A written apology and immediate payment in full of the fine in exchange for dismissing the contempt charge. Deal is accepted. Ms. Composed can now recompose and is finally history.

So, Who Will
Show Whom???

H E WAS A MAN IN his late forties or early fifties. By appearance and attitude, he was a want-to-be who never was and never would be and expressed his disappointment in life by seeking the opportunity to dispute and argue over any point he could. He was cited into court for excessive sound amplification from his motor vehicle. He had his stereo cranked up way too loud. An unusual citation for an individual of his advanced age. The recipients of that citation are more typically teenagers and people in their early twenties who have not yet determined that money can be invested in better things than sound systems in automobiles. However, we do not get to pick them; we just take them as they parade on into municipal court.

"Mr. Personum Importantus."

"I am here, sir," he responds. With a slow and deliberate stroll, he approaches the bench.

"Mr. Importantus, you are appearing on a citation for excessive sound amplification. How do you plead on the citation?"

Mr. Importantus, looking self-important and indignant, after a long pause and a sigh says, "I plead not guilty, Your Honor."

"Very well. The matter will be set for trial. You will be notified by mail of the date and time for trial. Make sure you appear at that time. The court will review any evidence you provide or consider any documents or witnesses you would like to present."

Mr. Importantus leaves. Time goes by, and it is now time for the trial of Mr. Importantus. He is present in the court with a smirk on his face throughout the proceedings leading up to his slot on the docket. When at last his turn is called, Mr. Importantus, carrying a handful of papers, approaches the bench.

"Mr. Importantus, are you ready to proceed?"

"Yes, Your Honor, I am ready to proceed."

The court: "Is the city ready to proceed?"

The officer: "Yes, Your Honor, the city is ready to proceed."

"Officer, raise your right hand and be sworn." Whereupon, the officer is sworn in and begins, "Your Honor, I was on duty in the city on blankety-blank date at that time in a marked patrol car, in full uniform, with my badge prominently displayed. As I was patrolling the neighborhood, I could hear music coming from some distance away. I could not see the vehicle. I would like the court to remember that this is late at night, sometime around 10:00 PM. It was in the summertime, so the window of my patrol car was down, but not only could I hear the vehicle coming, I could feel the base vibrating my car. As I rounded the corner onto Main Street, I observed Mr. Importantus in his vehicle coming toward me on Main Street. I determined that that was the car making the excessive noise. I turned around and pulled Mr. Importantus over and gave him a citation for excessive sound amplification. That is all I have, Your Honor."

"Mr. Importantus, do you have any questions of the officer?"

"No, I do not!"

"Very well, raise your right hand and be sworn." Whereupon Mr. Importantus is sworn in and invited to present his case.

"Your Honor, I was just listening to my music. This is a free country, and I ought to be able to listen to my music if I would like to. I had the windows rolled up, so it should not have been that loud outside of my car. I just think the officer did not have anything else to do and decided to give me a ticket."

"Why don't you tell me what kind of speakers you have in your car?"

Mr. Importantus, now delighted at the opportunity to brag about his toys, begins, "Well, Your Honor ..." and launches into a description of no less than twelve different speakers of various sizes.

"Mr. Importantus, of those speakers you described for me, how many are woofers or subwoofers and what size are they?"

"I have four woofers and two subwoofers. The woofers are all fourteen inches. There is one in each door, front and back, and the subwoofers are sixteen inches and they are mounted in the area behind the back seat."

"Mr. Importantus, what was the volume set on?"

"Well, Your Honor, I am a little hard of hearing so I did have the volume set up, but I had the windows up, too."

"Officer, how far away were you when you first heard the noise?"

"Your Honor, I was at least two and one-half blocks away when I heard Mr. Importantus coming."

"Very well. Based on the evidence, Mr. Importantus, I will find you guilty. However, this is your first infraction in this jurisdiction for this type of violation, so I will impose the minimum fine of $25. Can you pay that tonight?"

Mr. Importantus, now with a look of disgust says, "No, Your Honor, I cannot."

"Mr. Importantus, I will give you thirty days to have payment made in full. If you have not made payment in that time, you will need to come back into court to explain to me why you have not done so. Do you understand that?"

"Yes, Your Honor, I do." He turns and leaves the court.

About two weeks later when I arrive for an evening court, I am met by one of the clerks who has a grin across her face that would be most adequately described as an Alice In Wonderland Cheshire-Cat grin. On my desk is a letter. The letter is from Mr. Importantus. The letter advises the clerk that due to the injustice he feels he has suffered he does not feel he should have to pay the entire fine. Therefore, he has decided that he is only going to pay $24 of the $25 fine. Attached to the letter is a $24 check.

I am sorry, but I just cannot help it. Sometimes you just have to laugh out loud. This was not a complex legal problem. This was an issue of an idiot wanting to be a jerk and unfortunately making good progress in the effort. It took about a half a second for the court to decide on the next course of action for the solution of this challenge.

We waited until the thirty days had expired. At the first court date following the expiration of the thirty-day period, a warrant was ordered, signed, and entered. The warrant was for failure to pay a fine as scheduled. The court imposes a warrant fee of $25 every time we issue a warrant. I asked the clerk to send Mr. Importantus a letter advising him that due to his failure to pay the fine in full or appear in court as ordered, the court had issued a warrant for his arrest and that his obligation to the city was now $26, the remaining $1 from the initial fine and $25 for the warrant fee. The letter was mailed the next day. Within four days of the letter being sent, the court received an envelope from Mr. Importantus. This time there was no letter in the envelope, only a check for $26. The warrant was recalled. The balance bar of the scales of justice had now returned to level. Justice in its simplest form had prevailed yet once again.

Group IQ Is Not Cumulative, or Most Apples Fall Close to the Tree

I T HAS BEEN MY GOOD fortune to have truly excellent clerks throughout my tenure as a municipal court judge. The truth be told, if they, the clerks, were ventriloquists, they really would not need me. They deal with the individuals in their separate towns on a day-to-day basis. They therefore know the people very well and have their fingers firmly on the pulse of the community. They come to court with an expectation that I, the municipal court judge, will get things right. What a burden and a tough group to please.

They do contribute tremendously to the court's ability to be efficient and to minimize the time individuals spend before the court. They follow up to ensure everybody does what they are supposed to after court. Then, in their spare time, they are subjected to a barrage of angry phone calls, derogatory comments, and occasional threats from frustrated and angry individuals who have been inconvenienced by the irritation of a citation into court. On occasion, these individuals are irritated at the municipal court. That would be me.

On this particular day as I arrived in court, the clerk handed me a copy of a statute. She said, "You may want to read through this statute. It has been a while since you have seen one of these, and you have eighteen citations appearing for first appearances for violation of that statute."

The statute is entitled "Improper Positioning." Improper positioning is basically jaywalking. The statute provides that it is a violation for a pedestrian to walk on a road surface where traffic will travel if there is any other reasonable alternative, that is, a sidewalk, a shoulder, an unpaved open area where one could walk. The statute took all of about thirty seconds to review after which I inquired, "So, what's going on here?"

"Well," began the clerk, "we have had a problem with high school kids for several months now. Coming out of the high school toward the center of town, there is a narrow two-lane road with sidewalks on both sides. The high school students have decided that it is entertaining for them to walk in groups slowly down the center of the street and block traffic. We have gone to the high school, made announcements, and posted notices on bulletin boards. That has not done any good. The officers have talked to the kids, and the kids are ignoring them. We are now having the same problem all over town, as the high school kids think they can walk anywhere they want. So, in the last two weeks, the officers have issued eighteen citations for kids to appear here tonight. It is going to be a fun one tonight, isn't it?"

In this particular jurisdiction, we hold court three times a month. The two night sessions are held on Wednesday nights two weeks apart, and we hold an afternoon session on Tuesday afternoon on the week in between the two night sessions. This particular court session was a night session.

Not surprisingly, the courtroom was packed. We have our regulars who appear every other week for failure to make payments. We have new people appearing on new citations. On this particular night, we had a large group of high school age young adults accompanied by many friends and parents.

The docket drones on through first appearances. We reach a group of tickets that are paper clipped together. Yes, eighteen to be exact. All for "Improper Positioning." The only way to get through a list like this is to start, so we begin. I call the first name. A young lady, a junior or senior in high school, wearing pants that probably came out of a spray can or belonged to her younger sister and a pullover top that was likewise several sizes too small in an attempt to display that which she did not yet have and which nature may not ever give her. However, one must applaud the attempt. Her makeup is unusual and obviously applied by someone of either poor taste or inexperience. When I observe the adult female standing next to her, presumably her maternal unit, I understand why this child appears in public in the fashion in which she does. This apple did not fall far from the tree. The assault on my visual senses notwithstanding, the court and its work must move forward.

"Ms. Prissy, you are appearing on a violation of a statute for Improper Positioning. How do you plead?"

"I plead not guilty," she says quite dramatically, hands on hips, tossing her hair from side to side. Then she continues, "And I demand to have a trial with a jury."

"Ms. Prissy, we do not offer jury trials in this jurisdiction. If you had paid attention to the ordinance I reviewed at the beginning of court, you would have heard that. You will receive a trial before the court, which I will schedule. You will be mailed a trial notice with a date and time for the trial. Please bring any witnesses or evidence you would like to have the court review at that time."

I confirmed the address to which a written notice of the trial date would be sent and repeated the requirement that she would need to return at that time. Confirming that she understood those facts, I advised her she was through with the court and was free to leave. A glare from the mother did not warm the cockles of my heart. Although it did give me some indication as to what the general tenor of the trial might be like.

With seventeen more "Improper Positioning" citations waiting, I continue through the process. All seventeen entered not-guilty pleas and requested trials with varying degrees of ignorance, arrogance, humility, or fear. As the process continued, there were almost cheers for each teenager as a not-guilty plea was entered and the trial was scheduled.

With eighteen trials to be held, this would require a special setting. We elected to hold all of the trials on a Tuesday afternoon. The trials were scheduled, notices were sent out. With great anticipation, we awaited for the arrival of the date.

Due to the number of citations, the individuals involved, and the type of citations, the small-town newspaper had been present at the arraignment. The notoriety of the cases gained such standing as to merit a brief article printed in the county newspaper as well.

A couple of weeks before the scheduled trial date, not during a court session, a gentleman comes to City Hall and asks to speak to the court clerk. One of the clerks greets him at the counter. With some degree of pomposity, he takes out a business card, which he slides across the counter, and states, "My name is Mr. Prissy. I am Ms. Prissy's father. I am also the mayor of Nearby City (another small city some ten miles away. That small city's teenagers attend high school in this jurisdiction). I am here to get this whole matter straightened out and taken care of."

The clerk picks up the business card and looks at it. It identifies the gentleman as the mayor of the neighboring town. She looks at the card, looks at him, and inquires, "Sir, are you here as the mayor of the town, or are you here as the father for Ms. Prissy?"

After a momentary pause to think he responds, "Well, I guess I am here as the father of Ms. Prissy."

The clerk then places the card back on the counter and pushes it back toward the gentleman and says, "You will probably want to take this back, won't you?"

The conversation that ensues is neither friendly nor helpful, and after a few minutes, the mayor/father parental unit, despite his elevated status, leaves, recognizing that his daughter will have to appear in court at trial on this matter.

Our Tuesday afternoon court sessions are generally lightly attended. Only those people who are not at work or who prefer to appear at this time are present for this session. On this date the courtroom was full. Included in the audience were representatives from three different news stations. We take care of a few other preliminary matters and then get to the "Improper Positioning" citation trials.

The court calls the first case: "Ms. Prissy."

She stands. Straightens herself, tucks in stuff that is trying to get out, works her way through the crowd with a couple of giggles, winks at friends, and then sashays up to the designated location in the court. And … now … she speaks, "Your Honor, when I was cited, I was with my friend, Buffy. Buffy and I would like to have our cases heard at the same time. Can we do that?"

"Yes, ma'am. I believe we can consolidate those two matters to be heard at once." I turn to the police officer who is going to handle the case and inquire, "Officer, do you have any objection to consolidating these two cases?"

"No, sir, not at all. I would be glad to consolidate as many as they would like."

"Ms. Buffy, please approach the bench."

She stands, bats eyelashes, tosses hair, and joins Ms. Prissy. Though there is no family relationship or physical resemblance, the similarities are remarkable. Enough makeup to be on stage, but, oh well. The parents are easy to identify. Mr. and Mrs. Buffy and Mayor and Mrs. Prissy are glowing with pride as their progeny, the dynamic duo, are now prepared to defend freedom to walk in the street.

"Ms. Buffy, do you want your case to be heard with Ms. Prissy's?"

She giggles, covers her mouth with her hand, and then tossing her hair, inhales deeply and says, "Yes."

"Very well, let's proceed. Officer, can you raise your right hand and be sworn?" The officer is sworn in and begins.

"On blankety-blank day at approximately that time, I was on duty in the city in a marked patrol unit, in full uniform, badge prominently displayed. As I turned from Center Street onto Pine Street, Your Honor—that is the street that runs directly into the high school, about halfway up the block—I observed two young females walking down the center of the road. As I approached them, they did not move to get out of the way and continued walking directly down the center of the road. I then used my loudspeaker and asked them to step to the side of the road, which they did. I then cited both young ladies for Improper Positioning. The two young ladies that I cited are standing before the court. Ms. Prissy and Ms. Buffy. That is all I have at this time, Your Honor."

"Do either of you have any questions of the officer? This would be your opportunity to cross-examine this officer about anything he said."

Ms. Prissy, who is obviously in charge of the universe, speaks: "No, Your Honor, I do not have any questions of that officer. But he is totally wrong. It did not happen anything like that. It was totally different."

"Very well, raise your right hand and let me swear you in and you can tell me what happened."

Whereupon the witness is sworn in and … she begins.

"Well, my friend Buffy and I were walking down the side of the street on the sidewalk when we decided we wanted to cross over to the other side. So, right in the middle of the block, we walked in between two cars and started walking across the street diagonally. While we were walking across the street we were walking toward the high school. You know, we had to get back. It was almost after our lunch period, so we were hurrying, trying to get back to school and walking at an angle crossing the road. The officer pulled up behind us and seemed to be real impatient. He then turned on his loudspeaker, and he screamed at us. Your Honor, I am telling you he screamed at us to get off the road. So we stepped over to the edge of the road. Then he got out of his car and came over and he wrote us these tickets. He was very rude and mean to us." Voice trailing into a true whimper at the end there, complete with lower lip stuck out, droopy eyes, and almost tears. Bravo! What a performance.

"Well, let me see if I understand your testimony. You and your friend stepped out from between two cars and were crossing the street. However, instead of doing it in the shortest distance possible, which would be to cross the street at a right angle to the sidewalk, you were walking to cross the street on a diagonal angle."

"That is right, Your Honor. We were crossing the street but we were doing it at an angle."

"Well, at the angle you were walking, how far would it have taken you to get to the other side of the street? Would that have been half a block, a block, two blocks?"

"Well, Your Honor, it probably would have taken us most of the way to get to the high school." She looks at Buffy who nods in agreement.

"And if it was going to take you most of the way to get to the high school, then that would be approximately a block and a half to two blocks from where you stepped into the street. Is that correct?"

She thinks for a moment, her eyes roll up in her head, her

hands go on to her hips, and she says, "Well, that is probably about right."

"Very well. Thank you very much."

I then turn to Buffy. "You also have an opportunity to cross-examine the officer if you have anything you would like to ask him about."

Buffy has figured out that this is not going well. Buffy says, "No, Your Honor, I don't really have any questions of the officer."

"What would you like to tell me about this incident?"

"Your Honor, we were crossing the street like Ms. Prissy said, and we were walking at an angle, and it would have taken us quite a while to cross the street. But we were not intending to block traffic. We were just trying to cross the street."

"Thank you. Do either of you have anything else you would like to have the court consider?"

"No," responds Ms. Prissy, quite proud of her effort and confident about her possibility of success.

"No, Your Honor," responds Buffy.

"Very well. Officer, is there anything else you would like to have the court consider?"

"Your Honor, the only thing I would like to add is this is the first time I have heard that they were crossing the street at an angle. They made no mention of that to me at the time I issued them the citations."

"OK. Ms. Prissy, I have a couple more questions for you. It is my recollection that the road that leads from Main Street into the high school has sidewalks on both sides all the way. Is that accurate?"

"No, Your Honor. You are wrong, too. There is one section

on the south side of the road where the sidewalk is gone and it is just a dirt shoulder."

"So, there is either a sidewalk on one side of the road or a dirt shoulder and a sidewalk on the other side of the road, isn't there?"

"Yes, there is."

"Why do you not walk on the sidewalks?"

With Buffy now hanging her head and obviously fearing what Ms. Prissy might say, Ms. Prissy launches in to her explanation.

"Well, Your Honor, being as we all get out of school for lunch at the same time, there's a whole lot of kids trying to get off campus to go eat. There's also all of these kids in their cars trying to get off campus. Sometimes, you have to walk real slow because the people walking in front of you are not walking very fast. So, we sort of spill over out into the street and that way everyone can get off campus a lot sooner. I know it really makes the people in cars mad, but they need to understand that we are people, too. We are hungry, too. We deserve to have our lunch just as much as they do. Just because they have cars doesn't make them special."

"Got it. Based on the evidence before me, I will find you both guilty of Improper Positioning. The fact that there is a crowd on the sidewalk and it is not moving at the speed that you would like is not a reason for you to block traffic in the road. We will impose the minimum fine of $45. How do you propose to pay the fine?"

At this point, a man in the audience stands up and speaks in a loud and pompous voice, "Your Honor, may I be heard?" This is the mayor from the neighboring city. Ms. Prissy before me is his darling daughter. Connecting the dots is always helpful in getting the whole picture.

"Sir, it would be unusual to allow you to appear if you are not an attorney representing one of the defendants in this case. However, what would you like to tell me?"

Mr. Prissy bulls his way through the audience, stepping on people as he comes. He approaches the bench and stands by his daughter. Who then, bolstered by the arrogance of her self-appointed important father, becomes even more indignant. Mr. Prissy begins, "I don't think this is right. These kids were not intending to do anything wrong. The city is just picking on them, trying to make money on those of us that do not live here in this city. We are not going to take this lying down. We are going to appeal this ticket all the way to the Supreme Court if we have to."

"Well sir, your daughter has appeal rights, which you are entitled to exercise. Appeals have to be filed with the circuit court down at the county courthouse. Absent an appeal being filed, I expect the fines to be paid or arrangement made for payment. If the fines are not paid within thirty days of today, your daughter will need to appear at the next scheduled court date to explain why not. Do you understand that?"

"Yes, I do," she says indignantly. They turn on their heels and leave the courtroom.

There is a moment of silence as the reality of the situation now settles in over the remaining sixteen parties. The group mentality that they had enjoyed in the parking lot of "we are right" and "we will not stand for this" seems to have diminished just a little.

I call the next case. Mr. Nextinline, a young man in the

upper grades of high school, stands and politely works his way through the crowd up to the front.

"Sir, are you ready to proceed?" the court asks.

"Yes, sir, I am," he states.

"Officer, you are still under oath. You may proceed."

"Well, Your Honor, on blankety-blank day at that time, I was on patrol in the city in a clearly marked patrol car, in full uniform with badge prominently displayed. I had a ride-along with me that day who is a reporter from the local newspaper. She is present and will testify in a moment. We had been at the high school because she was doing a newspaper article on high school kids driving to school. As we left the school, and, Your Honor, this was while class was in session, there was a group of eight high school kids blocking the entire road as we were on the road leading from the high school to Main Street. I pulled up behind them, and none of them turned around to look at the vehicle and all continued to walk, blocking the entire roadway. I then activated my loudspeaker and requested that they all move off the road on the south side and line up by the fence so that I could issue them citations. They were surprised to see a police officer when they turned around, but they complied and lined up by the fence. I then parked my car along the edge of the road and began writing tickets. As I was writing the fourth or fifth ticket, the individual I was writing the ticket for pointed out into the street and said there were three more kids walking out in the street and then asked, 'Why don't you get them?' I turned around and observed three more individuals walking in the street. I then invited them to join us in the line at the fence and I issued them all citations."

I turn to Mr. Nextinline, "Mr. Nextinline, do you have any questions about anything the officer said?"

Mr. Nextinline shakes his head and says, "No, Your Honor, I don't think so."

Back to the officer. "Officer, you have a witness?"

"Yes, Your Honor. We would call Ms. Reporter."

Ms. Reporter approaches the bench and stands by the officer.

"Ms. Reporter, do you solemnly swear to tell the truth, the whole truth, and nothing but the truth?"

"Yes, Your Honor, I do."

"Go ahead. What did you see?"

"Your Honor, just like the officer said. As we were trying to leave the high school this group of young people were in the road. The officer pulled up behind them, and we followed them for a few seconds hoping that they would move. None of them did. They all just refused to turn around and even look at the vehicle though they clearly could hear it. The officer then asked them to stand by the fence, and he wrote them all citations. I was standing by the front of the car when the one young man pointed to the other three students who were walking down the road. The officer then asked them to join in the lineup by the fence, and they were all issued citations."

"Were there any other students present at the time where there would be any confusion about which students were in the road and which students were given citations?"

"No, Your Honor. School was in session, and I am not sure why these students were not in school."

"Mr. Nextinline, do you have any questions for this witness?"

Mr. Nextinline: "No, Your Honor, I don't."

"Mr. Nextinline, raise your right hand and be sworn." Mr. Nextinline is sworn in and the court continues, "Go ahead. What would you like to tell me?"

"Well, Your Honor, we were walking off school, and I guess we were in the road. However, I was right by the curb. I was the first one nearest the edge of the curb on the side of the street where the officer made us stand to give us the tickets. I could not have been out in the road more than a couple of feet or three feet at most. I do not think it is fair that we all got tickets. They probably should have given us a warning or something. That is all I have to say, Your Honor."

"Officer, anything else you would like for the court to consider?"

"Well, Your Honor, there was a group of the eight of them that were in the road, and the nearest one to the curb on either side would have been four to five feet away. They were not in a straight line together, but they were in a group and they blocked the entire center of the roadway."

"Thank you, Officer. Based on the evidence, sir, I will find you guilty. I will also impose a minimum fine. Do you intend to appeal this matter? I hope you heard my instructions to the last defendants."

"Yes, Your Honor."

The court then turns to the remainder of the docket. "Ladies and gentlemen, there should be ten more of you out there that were in this group of eleven that were cited on this day. Would you please stand and approach the bench."

Ten young people rise. About an equal mixture of boys

and girls form one large group. The court puts them all under oath and turns to the officer.

"Officer, would your testimony in regard to these ten defendants be any different from what you told before?"

"No, Your Honor, it would not."

"Ms. Reporter, would your testimony in regard to these ten defendants be substantially different in any way from what you previously told me?"

"No, Your Honor, it would not."

"Very well. Do any of you have any questions for the officer or for Ms. Reporter?" There are no takers on this opportunity, so I continue, "Is there anything any of the ten of you would like to tell me, and I might say that needs to be one at a time, about the events that happened that give rise to the citations?"

A couple of them make statements regarding lack of notice of the law, but basically everybody agrees on the facts. This expedites the matter and all ten are found guilty and minimum fines are imposed across the board. By this time, I have several parents standing. One very angry lady makes reference to Nazis and the Gestapo. An opinionated, rather large man with his beer belly hanging out from under the bottom of a T-shirt that is too short, makes statements about the city trying to get rich off the backs of the citizens. They all vow to appeal. I instruct them with regard to their appeal rights and how to pursue those and move on to the remainder of the cases.

The fifteenth defendant is called and approaches the bench with a large man who is obviously a farmer or a rancher who has been working. He is dirty. That honest dirty that comes from doing real hard work. He holds a hat in his hand, sports a farmer's tan—a tan line mid-forehead where his hat would cover his head, and dark tanned cheeks, face, and neck. I am betting this is a father.

The father is going to speak.

I begin, "Sir, it is your son's citation, and it is unusual to allow representation unless you are an attorney in this court. If you would like to stand there and support your son, I would be glad to allow you to do that. I will also give you an opportunity to speak later, assuming that you are his father."

The gentleman begins, "Your Honor, I have spoken to my son already. He has something he would like to say to you."

"Go ahead. What would you like to say?"

The son speaks, "Well, Your Honor, I was standing in the street, and I would like to change my not-guilty plea to guilty if I can do that. I am sorry that I did that and I will never do it again."

Father nods his head with approval, looks down at his son, and then turns and looks at me and gives a slight nod.

"I will accept your change of plea to guilty. I will also impose a minimum fine of $45. You have been in court, so you have heard that you will need to have a payment made in thirty days or be back in court to explain why not."

The father interrupts, "Your Honor, I will pay the fine right now, but he will work it off for me. I can assure you, this will never happen again. I apologize for my son's behavior."

With the dignity of responsible human beings, father and son approach the clerk where the father hands over the cash to pay for his son's fine. He then puts his arm around the young man's shoulder, and they exit the court, exuding the quiet dignity of having accepted responsibility for the indiscretions of youth and teaching an important lesson to a son who knows his father cares about him.

What a contrast from the other seventeen young people and their parents. After this experience, I wished there was a way to impose the fine and the penalty on the parents.

There were articles in the local city and county paper the next day. The newspaper described it as an attempt by eighteen darling children to defend themselves against a small-town police department and court. It was stated that the court politely and courteously crushed each attempt at defense. Oh well.

*   *   *

Time went by. The court clerk talked to the clerk in circuit court. Several of the parents did march down to the county court with their children to file their appeals. When they discovered that the filing fee for the appeal was almost double what the fine was, they expressed their opinion as to the inequity of the judicial system and stormed out. Shortly after that, payments started to appear at the clerk's office.

On or about the twenty-eighth day after court, the mayor's daughter, Ms. Prissy, came in to see the court clerk. She approached the counter and arrogantly announced that she was there to pay her fine. She placed a glass jar partially filled with coins on the counter. There was a note taped to the jar requesting donations to help this poor young lady fight the injustice of the police and the court. The jar was about half full of coins.

The clerk did not blink or show any expression on her face. She simply took the lid off the jar, poured the coins out on the counter, and began arranging the coins in one-dollar stacks. When that task was done, the clerk counted forty-five one-dollar stacks and then prepared a receipt for Ms. Prissy. There were a few coins left on the counter. The clerk then carefully and politely placed the excess coins back in the jar, put the lid on, returned the jar to Ms. Prissy, and thanked her. Dignity and class in the face of disrespect is hard to beat. There were seventeen young people who learned from their parents through this experience that the rules and laws of society may or may not apply to them, based on their opinion at the time. One young man did receive good counsel, advice, and support from a father who actually cared about his son's upbringing. One can only hope that given time, the younger generation will mature and grow beyond their genetic and environmental examples and, with any luck, there will have been a genetic mutation in a favorable direction so that these young people will outgrow and become better citizens than the examples their parents have set.

Sometimes, the Words Are Worth a Thousand Pictures

ONE OF THE OPTIONS OFFERED to offenders of the traffic laws is an "appearance by letter." When an individual contacts the court and requests to appear by letter, the clerk of the court always advises the person that several things are required to be in the letter for it to be sufficient for a first appearance in the Court.

First, you must enter a plea. The options are: guilty, not guilty, or no contest. Without a plea, the court is unable to efficiently move forward with disposition of the citation.

Second, you may provide the court with an explanation of the circumstances or facts that you want the court to consider either during trial or in the imposition of a penalty if you plead guilty or are found guilty after a trial on the merits of the case.

Third, if a guilty or no-contest plea is entered, some information about your ability to pay a fine is helpful to assist the court in setting a workable payment schedule.

The courts have received many letters. Writing skills, state of mind, experiences with the police officer, general feelings about traffic laws, general state of the author's life all come into play as authors set pen to paper or finger to keyboard to present their case. What follows is one of my all-time favorite letters. It is presented in content as close as I can recall, including misspellings and punctuations, to preserve the uniqueness of the letter and give the reader a similar experience that I had the evening I read the letter for the first time.

It was a speeding ticket. The charge alleged that the driver was going sixty-five miles per hour in a posted zone of fifty-five miles per hour. The bail amount on the ticket was $130. The hand-printed letter read as follows:

To: Whom it may Concern,9-3-XX

I am writing in regards to the Traffic Citation I recieved on Aug, 1 of XX. I was driving a 92 Geo Metro with a 1.0 liter 3 cylinder Engine and was Ironiclly cited for speeding. I tend to believe driving a car in this horse power range was punnishment enough, but apparently not. I was traveling approximatlly 65 in a 55 on a 2 lain Highway (name of highway) at a time of night where traffic was minimal. Personally, I feel this was a judgment Call for the officer and honestly I think he made the wrong judgment. I'm 20 years old, I have Car payments, Ins, misc. bills, I basiclly support my self. I underStand I was traveling faster than the posted speed limit but I trully do not believe I deserve a 130.00 Ticket, beside I can't afford it either,

113

To top it all off I recentlly found out my girlfriend is pregnent and at the time I was pulled over she had on wet clothes. My driver side window was broken down, the heater didn't work, she was freezing, and prier to being pulled over I had stopped twice to warm her up. I had explained this to the officer but he didn't seen to care. In conclusion I would like to say that I'm the type of person that can learn just as much from a warning than a $130.00 fine. I urge you to take these things into concideration when making your judgment.

Thank you for your Time,

Sincerely,

A specific plea was not stated—nowhere did he say guilty or not guilty. So the court took the admission of exceeding the speed limit as a guilty plea, since if the matter was heard at trial that would have been the outcome. This point was explained to the defendant in a letter that was sent in response to the letter the court had received. The defendant was also advised that if he disagreed with the court's decision he could contact the court.

The court is familiar with many defenses to speeding tickets. A review of the statute confirmed my long-time understanding as to the available defenses. Unfortunately, there was no "pregnent," cold girlfriend defense. Likewise, there was no "Geo Metro, broken down window" exception or defense, though I did have some sympathy for the general concept.

The evaluation process being complete, the court

determined that a fine was in order. Then, taking exception to the heartfelt opinion that one can learn as much from a warning as from a fine, the court imposed the minimum fine.

The minimum fine was substantially less than $130, seeking the balance between learning from a warning and having that learning reinforced by a modest fine. No, I have no clue what process was used to warm a cold, "pregnent" girlfriend in a Geo Metro with a broken window with no heater. All in all, we learned more than we thought we needed to or really wanted to.

A Penalty Earned Saved Nothing

L OGIC AND REASON ARE INTERESTING skills or capabilities. What might seem perfectly reasonable and sane under one set of circumstances can quickly move into the ridiculous or the "you've got to be kidding" insane arena. Frequently, an uncontrolled or self-declared uncontrollable emotional state can taint the human's capacity to use logic or reason. An after-the-fact review, a postmortem, as it were, can be beneficial. You know, viewing one's actions in retrospect from a less emotionally burdened perspective can give one a totally different view.

Anger, irritation, or an assault on the sensitive center of one's being tend to move some people away from the logical and reasonable by somehow enhancing the ability to rationalize through a thought process that, at best, can be called ... let's see ... oh, yeah ... foolish.

Criminal mischief. An infrequent citation, but when it appears, it is generally accompanied by interesting facts. The face of the citation creates interest due to the lack of information. Criminal mischief. That is all the citation will say. Not a clue as to the action on which the citation is based. So, when these citations appear and a guilty plea is entered, the person cited to appear always gets to explain the course of events that led to his or her path's crossing with mine. This is one such case.

"Mr. Honestlyregretful," calls the court.

"Yes, sir," he responds, standing and moving to the front of the courtroom. He is tall, very average looking, moderately clean and presentable, in his midtwenties, with a sheepish grin on his face and an air of embarrassment exuding from the unsure manner in which he moves. His eyes look around the courtroom filled with other involuntary participants, hoping not to see anyone one he knows and wishing his name had come up later on the docket.

"Sir, you are appearing on a citation for criminal mischief. How do you plead?"

"Well … hummmm … I would be guilty, Your Honor."

"Very well, please tell me what you did."

"OK," he sighs, inhales, and begins, "I slashed my ex-girlfriend's car tires."

"Why did you do that?"

Another deep sigh and here it comes. "See, my ex-girlfriend had been accusing me of slashing her car tires and was demanding that I pay her for the tires. I had not touched her tires. But she kept saying that I had and insisting that I pay for the tires. I went over to see if I could straighten the situation out. She kept screaming at me and telling me that I was going to pay for the tires. So I said, 'If I am going to have to pay for some tires, I might as well slash them.' So, I did."

"Now that you are here today and have had a chance to think about it, how are you feeling about it now?"

"It probably was not the best choice, was it?"

"I think we can agree on that point. Is there anything else you would like me to consider before I impose a fine?"

"No, sir, I don't think so."

Thereafter, a fine was imposed and restitution was ordered. Mr. Honestlyregretful looked relieved as he left the courtroom. He had acknowledged his moment of indiscretion and foolishness and would pay the penalty. I doubt it is a story he will tell with pride to his children or neighbors. It seems that, more often than not, in this type of case, an "ex" something or other is always involved.

DIRTY AND JUSTICE
JUST DO NOT MIX

WITHIN MY FIRST FEW WEEKS on the bench, an interesting phenomenon became evident. Individuals with extensive driving records that would deserve large fines would advise the court that they were not employed. By being unemployed, they had no income and therefore had no way to pay a fine. This became known as "The Poverty Appeal." It performed the function of an appeal from the court's decision to the perceived higher laws of nature in that one could not get blood from a turnip. It also became somewhat obvious that these individuals could afford tobacco, drove cars, got tattoos, purchased six, twelve, twenty-four, and forty-eight packs of beer, and yet did not seem to lose weight or even appear to suffer from lack of nutrition. All of this could happen without any income. The obvious problem here was that these people did not want to have the resources to pay their fines. By simply denying the ability to pay, they were able to not pay.

One evening after court, as the bailiff, clerks, and I were discussing the situation, we came upon a possible solution.

It was immediately dubbed "pay or appear." Pay or appear relies on the theory that if the defendant is not working, then he and/or she can come to the court two or three times a month and reaffirm that they are not working and that they have no money and cannot pay. Legal research over the next couple of days confirmed that the court had the ability to order continued appearances and not violate any statutory or constitutional rights. Thus, the very next court date, our pay-or-appear plan was implemented.

That night, many individuals who appeared before the court either pled guilty or were found guilty after a trial. The poverty appeal was then offered. The pay-or-appear plan was then the counteroffer. At first, this new opportunity seemed to confuse the clientele. When the realization of what would be required set in, it would elicit a question. The immediate question was how long the pay-or-appear plan would continue. The court was prepared for this and responded with, "Until your fine is paid in full." The next question was also anticipated, that question being, "Do you expect me to leave work to come to court?" The answer to that question was, "No. Never leave work to come to court for pay-or-appear. However, if you are at work, your employer will need to provide confirmation that you are employed and present at work during the time court is in session." Since most court sessions occur in the evening, the likelihood of conflict was minimal.

There are also those individuals who have managed to avoid many of life's consequences by inflicting upon those who would impose a consequence a long diatribe of explanations and excuses. They fancy themselves as being able to talk their way out of anything. Some are gifted and skilled, while others are merely voluminous and irritating.

On to the facts of this chapter. This was an average evening. The court was in session, droning on through the docket. Mr. Gotcha's name is called. Mr. Gotcha is a man slight of build, with sandy blonde hair with some gray, which is not terribly noticeable. He has a very bushy mustache, and is in his late forties to middle fifties, slender, short … wirey, I guess you would have to say. When his name is called, he rises, and with some degree of swagger and bravado approaches the bench. Hands shoved into front pockets of jeans, moving in slow motion, chewing what is presumably chewing gum, but one never knows. Attitude is one of incensed at having to be there, of righteous indignation over the humiliation and the loss of time from other preferred endeavors.

"Mr. Gotcha, you are appearing on two citations tonight. First citation is driving while suspended, and the second citation is for driving without insurance. How do you plead, sir?"

Mr. Gotcha shakes his head, jaw still twitching, finally looks up at the court, and says, "Well, Your Honor, my license was suspended. However, I was in a situation where I had to drive."

"I will be glad to listen to any extenuating circumstances, but at this point in the proceeding, the court needs you to enter a plea. Your options are guilty or not guilty, or no contest."

"Well, Your Honor, I guess I would have to say that technically I was guilty, I suppose." Thereafter follows a large sigh and a rolling of the eyes.

"Mr. Gotcha, since you entered a guilty plea, I can now

entertain any explanation you would have for justifying your operation of the vehicle with a suspended license and without insurance."

And he begins, "Your Honor, I really had no choice. I had to drive. I had an emergency situation that I had to take care of. My friend who had gone up to get a load of firewood was on his way back into town. He threw a rod about two miles out of town. He called me on his cell phone and told me he could not afford to have the vehicle towed. He tried to call everybody else he could think of and was not able to find anybody that would come and tow his truck on into town. Well, I was always taught that if someone needs your help, you should help them. I knew I would be driving very carefully. I knew I would take no chances to make sure no one got hurt. So, I got into my pickup and drove out to pull his truck into town. It was kind of late in the day, and it was just starting to get dark when I got out there. We got him hooked up with a chain and just as we were getting back into town, a police officer pulled us over because he said I did not have my lights turned on and it was too dark. When he asked for my license, I told him I did not have it with me. So, he ran my name through the computer and it came back that my driver's license was suspended. Nobody got hurt by this, Your Honor. I was just helping a friend get his truck back into town. I think the ticket should be dismissed because I was doing something good for somebody who needed it."

"Mr. Gotcha, you also were aware you did not have insurance?"

"Yeah, I knew I did not have insurance."

"I am now reviewing your driving record. You do have

an extensive driving record. You have received numerous citations for everything from speeding to driving while suspended. While your intentions may have been to help a friend, you should consider that compliance with state laws regarding operator's license and insurance should be met before you undertake such activities."

The court imposes a fine, which is substantial.

At this point, Mr. Gotcha becomes very indignant, "Your Honor, I do not believe that is fair. That is an awful lot of money to make me pay because I was helping a friend."

"Sir, the court is not seeking your agreement or consent for the amount of the fine. As I told you, I appreciate your effort to assist a friend. However, you should choose the manner in which you are going to assist people so that it does not require you to violate the law. I will set payments for you at $100 a month. Your first payment will be due thirty days from now, and the payments of $100 a month will continue until you get the fine paid. Do you understand that?"

"Yeah, I understand that, but I do not think this is fair and I cannot pay. I am not working. I may be out on a disability, so I am not gonna pay."

Ah. The appeal of poverty launched in its finest form. However, this will only be the next in a long stream of appeals of poverty the court will encounter with this Mr. Gotcha. The court is prepared.

"Very well, Mr. Gotcha. You will be appearing in court three times a month until you are able to start making the payments that have been ordered by the court. Do you understand that?"

"What do you mean? I have to keep coming to court?"

"That would be correct. Your next appearance date will be two weeks from tonight at 7:00 PM. However, if you make your payment before that time, you do not have to appear."

"I don't think this is fair—"

The court interrupts, "Mr. Gotcha, the court is through with you for this evening. Your opinion as to the fairness or equity of the situation is irrelevant to me. There are other matters on the docket to attend to. Either make your payment within the next two weeks or appear in court as ordered. That will be all."

Mr. Gotcha shakes his head in disbelief. He throws his hands in the air and, with a great deal of indignation, leaves the courtroom.

Two weeks go by. Mr. Gotcha is present. When his name is called, the court inquires whether he is able to make payment. When Mr. Gotcha advises the court the payments will not be forthcoming, he is ordered to appear again on the next court date. This process is repeated three times a month for about the next five or six months.

Prior to this time frame, purely by happenstance, the city had purchased a grocery store that had gone out of business. The building was remodeled and converted into a new city hall. This increased space for the city offices by about six- to tenfold. At significant expense, the city had built a nice city council chambers, which included a raised bench behind which the mayor and city council would sit during city council meetings.

As in the old city hall, the court uses city council chambers as a courtroom on court nights. The new courtroom includes comfortable chairs for the mayor and city council and nice padded chairs for the audience. The chairs are the straight-backed version, with fabric on the seat and the back. Three rows of chairs fill the audience/gallery part of the courtroom.

About the second or third time court was held in this new facility, Mr. Gotcha shows up at court covered—no, saturated—in grease and motor oil. Obviously, he has been working on a vehicle. His intent in coming to court is an ill-advised act of defiance to show disrespect to the court. I do not notice Mr. Gotcha's filthy condition until partway through the evening. When his name is called, the conversation goes something like this.

"Mr. Gotcha."

"Yeah, Your Honor, I am here."

He approaches the bench.

"Mr. Gotcha, you appear as though you have at least been near work. I make that observation based on the soiled condition of your clothes."

"Yeah, I have been helping my friend change out a transmission in his truck. I did not have time to change, so I came like this."

"Mr. Gotcha, if you have the time and ability to do mechanical work, you should seek employment."

"I am still working on my disability."

"Well, if you're physically able to do mechanical work, it certainly raises a question in my mind as to the degree of your disability. Furthermore, the court would appreciate your taking some effort to have yourself at least minimally clean so as not to offend others who are around you. That will be all for tonight. You will need to appear two weeks from tonight at 7:00 PM unless you are able to make a payment by then."

"Well, Your Honor, I guess I will just have to keep showing up forever because I am never gonna pay you. I am never gonna make any payments here."

"Very well. We will continue to see you until such time as you comply with the court's orders."

After court that evening, the bailiff noticed that the seat on which Mr. Gotcha had been sitting was stained from the oil and grease that had been on his clothing. The discussion ensued as to a remedy for this disrespect for city property and the court. Someone made a recommendation to cite Mr. Gotcha for destruction of city property, criminal mischief, or other such charges. It was my belief that those consequences would do nothing more than encourage Mr. Gotcha to continue the same behavior.

Two weeks later, the police officers who attend court had been requested to contact Mr. Gotcha before he entered the courtroom and to keep Mr. Gotcha standing at the end of the bench.

As court began, Mr. Gotcha was the first person called.

"Mr. Gotcha, the officers were requested by the court to detain you before you could sit in the courtroom. Last time, when you were here, you were filthy, dirty, and covered with grease. You stained and cause damage to one of the new chairs that are in the courtroom. Fortunately, maintenance was able to clean the chair, so there has been no permanent damage. However, your lack of respect for city property and to the court has been duly noted. To prevent future conduct of this kind, there has been a place identified for you in the back corner of the courtroom. From now on, when you arrive at court, you are to take position in your place. Your place has been designated by a small 'x' made of masking tape that has been placed on the carpeting in the back corner of the courtroom. Although the tape will not remain after tonight, that is your spot. Each and every time you appear in this court, you are to stand on your spot. You will remain standing on that spot until your name is called. Once you have completed your business with the court, you are required to leave the building so you do not cause any further damage to city property. Do you understand what I am telling you, sir?"

"Do you mean I have to stand back there in the corner?"

"That is correct, Mr. Gotcha. The 'x' has been placed far enough away from both of the walls so that you will not touch the wall and there are no chairs in that aisle. You will stand on that spot during your time here in court. If you do not appear in court, or if you do not stand on the spot as ordered by the court, you will be found in contempt of court and will be lodged in the county jail. Do you understand that?"

Mr. Gotcha stands silent and glares.

So the court continues, "Very well. If we're clear on that point, Mr. Gotcha, please go to the back of the courtroom. The officer will show you where your spot is and you are to stand there, facing the court, so we can keep track of you while you are here."

Mr. Gotcha moves to the back of the courtroom, stands on his spot, places his hands in his pockets, and begins to glare at me. If looks could kill, my wife would have collected life insurance and would be living the life to which she is so richly entitled. This was a strong indication that the solution had been effective and accomplished the desired goal. I then took the next step of making sure that Mr. Gotcha was one of the last names I called each night. The longer Mr. Gotcha stood on the spot, the angrier he became.

Mr. Gotcha continued to stand on his spot for a couple of months. And then it happened. Mr. Gotcha did not appear in court as ordered. A warrant was issued.

The court at which I preside is in a very, very small town. The city police not only know almost everybody in town, but they know where they live. Furthermore, they know if they work, where they work, and when they work. They know their wives, their mothers, their sisters, their brothers, their children who are in school, what grades those children are in, and the grades they get or do not get. Thus, executing a warrant is seldom a problem. When the warrant was issued that night, several officers stood in line and flipped a coin to see who would get to execute the warrant on Mr. Gotcha.

Two weeks later, when I returned to court, I inquired as to what happened with the warrant and Mr. Gotcha. I was advised by the police officers that Mr. Gotcha was very surprised when the police officers showed up to arrest him on a warrant for failure to appear. Mr. Gotcha really did not want to go to jail. Mr. Gotcha had inquired as to whether there was any alternative to jail. He was advised by the officer that he could post bail as stated on warrant. The bail was set on the warrant so that the minimum payment the defendant could post as bail would satisfy all outstanding fines, warrants, fees, and penalties to the city. Mr. Gotcha posted, in cash, full payment of his fine.

The court is not one to gloat; well, at least not much. However, there is a warm and fuzzy feeling of satisfaction that comes over one when goals are met, objectives achieved, and justice served. Ah, the sweet taste of success.

You Earned the Right How??

REMEMBERING MY PREVIOUSLY EXPRESSED OPINION with regard to the effectiveness of the temperance movement and legislation that addresses issues that arise from the operation of motor vehicles while under or near the influence of alcohol, we are back to another "open container" case. The open-container statute prohibits an open container of an alcoholic beverage in a motor vehicle within the reach of the driver. This is a citation that generally comes accompanied by a speeding ticket, an unlawful turn, and/or failure to obey a traffic-control device. The officer will pull the individual over for some other reason and as the officer approaches the vehicle, he or she will observe an open beer, wine bottle, or hard liquor container. There are those rare occasions when the Neanderthals who have not quite caught up to the societal norms for the consumption of alcohol will openly and blatantly drink while they drive. Thus, an officer in close proximity has an excellent view of the container from which the Neanderthal is drinking while they are driving. This is one such case.

As his name is read, he works his way from the back of the crowd that fills the courtroom. Average in height, slightly overweight, mostly around the midriff; you know, the bulging belly that presses the belt buckle forward to where it is pointing out at about a forty-five-degree angle from true vertical. Salt-and-pepper hair, three-day-old growth of beard, ashen skin color, probably a smoker. He meanders slowly across the courtroom up to the appointed spot.

The court begins, "Mr. Unevolved, you are appearing tonight on a citation for an open container in a motor vehicle. How do you plead?"

"Well, Your Honor, I am guilty."

"Thank you, Mr. Unevolved, for your plea. Now, were you aware that it is a violation of the law to have an open container of alcohol in your vehicle?"

"Yes, Your Honor, I was aware of that."

"What type of beverage were you drinking?"

"It was a beer, Your Honor. It was a good, cold beer after a long, hard day of work."

"Very well. Mr. Unevolved, is there anything you'd like to say to the court before I impose penalty?"

"Nope, that's about it, Your Honor. Just having a quick, cold one after a long hard day of work."

At this point, I review the driving record. Mr. Unevolved has an extensive driving record, including a couple of driving under the influence convictions, several speeding tickets, and two other citations for an open container within the last four and a half years.

"Mr. Unevolved, due to your extensive driving record and your previous violations of this statute the court will impose the maximum fine of $___."

The dollar amount of the fine elicits a "whooa" from the

audience in the courtroom. Mr. Unevolved's eyes finally snap open. He stares at the bench in disbelief.

Shaking his head he says, "Wow, that's pretty stiff, don't you think, Your Honor?"

"I regret that I am limited by statute and that that is the highest fine I can impose under the law. It seems that you do not believe that the traffic laws of this state apply to you. You need to be advised that each and every time you appear before this court on this or any other citation, I will impose maximum fines. Do you understand that?"

"Yes, Your Honor."

Whereupon, payment arrangements are made and Mr. Unevolved turns to leave the courtroom, and as he passes by the officer who is acting as bailiff that evening, he looks him in the eye, shrugs his shoulders and says, "Damn, that was the wrong answer, wasn't it?" and leaves the courtroom.

Somehow, there is a misguided belief that is somewhat pervasive through a certain segment of our society. The belief that an unspecified number of good deeds then entitles the individual to free opportunity to violate the law. While Mr. Unevolved may have had a long, hard day, and a nice, cold beer would have been very satisfying, perhaps he will make a better selection of a time and place to consume the beer next time. However, one never knows. The process of education is much more difficult to some people than to others. The influence of alcohol tends to extend rather than shrink that overall time period.

It Just Is Not Over until Mama Says It Is Over

THE HUMAN BEING IS A complex creature. Not only is the human being a complex creature, it associates with other human beings who are likewise complex creatures. Though I give it my best effort as a new Mr., Mrs., or Ms. Someone appears before me, it is not possible to discern from the visual appearance all those things that may or may not be going on in their lives. There are no clues as to relationships, or lack thereof, level of sophistication, or lack thereof, or to what extent their lives are directed or controlled. Thus, the court tends to take people at face value. Appearance, demeanor, attitude, and age all play into the court's attempt to find that always elusive, and never unanimously agreed upon, point at which justice is best served.

Ordinary court night. Court is working its way through first-appearance tickets when the court gets to a common, run-of-the-mill, vanilla-flavored speeding ticket. The ticket is a speeding ticket for doing forty-five in a twenty-five. No big deal? Right.

Court calls Ms. Dainty. Ms. Dainty stands, works her way to the front of the courtroom through the crowd of people that are still waiting for their turn to be heard. Ms. Dainty is young. Very young. I review the ticket to confirm that she is at least sixteen years of age. And in fact she is. Just a few months past her sixteenth birthday. Ms. Dainty is giggling as if she is either not taking this matter seriously or nervous. Finally, she gains control of herself and smiles. She is reasonably well dressed and groomed, behaving somewhat like a giddy schoolgirl. But then she is only sixteen, right?

The court begins, "Ms. Dainty, you are appearing on a speeding ticket, doing forty-five in a twenty-five. How do you plead?"

Ms. Dainty giggles, "Tee hee hee, well, Your Honor, I could see the forty-five-mile-per-hour speed limit, and I was just speeding up because I knew I was going to go that fast. The officer explained to me that I was not supposed to go that fast until I got to the sign. But I did not realize that before that—*giggle giggle*. So, I guess I'm—*pause*—well, I guess I'm guilty. I do have a clean driving record, though, if that counts for anything."

"Yes, ma'am, a good driving record will influence the penalty I will impose as a result of your guilty plea. You have not been driving very long, have you?"

"No, sir, I just got my license a couple months ago."

"Well, ma'am, due to the short period of time you have had your driver's license, I would expect you to have a relatively clean driving record and you, in fact, do. This is your first speeding ticket, isn't it?"

"Yeah, this is my first ticket."

"Very well. I will impose the minimum fine of ___ dollars. Can you pay tonight?"

She looks back at an adult female sitting in the back of the courtroom. Obviously a parental unit, presumably a mother. Mother nods with a disgusted look on her face and moves to the front of the courtroom to write a check to pay the clerk to satisfy the fine. While the check is being written and the receipt being issued, the court continues on with other cases and pays no more attention to Ms. Dainty and her mother. They quietly leave the courtroom.

At this point, you would think that is the end of this story and that it was pretty boring I know. I thought it was. But no, not this time. What follows is a copy of a letter from Ms. Dainty's mother. Obviously disappointed with the court's ruling, she felt the need to express her disappointment in written form. The names have been changed to protect the innocent and not to embarrass those worthy of embarrassment as a result of this letter. The letter, on business letterhead from a real estate office with a business card attached, read as follows:

Dear Judge:

On October 19th my daughter Ms. Dainty was pulled over by Officer S.F. (think that is his name, his handwriting is hard to read) for speeding. He wrote on the citation that he clocked her speeding 44 mph in a 25 mph zone at Bridgeport, and she was going West on Stevens Road. She was approximately 100 yards from the sign indicating that the speed limit was changing to 45 mph. The officer followed my daughter for a little bit, as she did not see him and has never been pulled over by a police officer before. In talking with my daughter, we arrived at the conclusion that this angered the officer. When she did pull over roadside, she broke down in tears, as she was petrified that something bad had happened.

My point in writing this letter is this was her very first traffic stop, couldn't the officer have explained how you shouldn't accelerate up to a traffic sign, but wait until you get there and then it is legal to drive the speed that the sign designates? Couldn't he have given her a warning? Most every new driver (she got her license in June) makes a mistake in their first year. Where is the compassion for our youth? It isn't like she is driving an old vehicle with expired tags, and tail lights not working. She had a clean record (as he very well knew), and is a great kid, doesn't skip school, drink alcohol, take drugs, or ever miss her curfew. I don't understand how he could look at a sobbing 16-year-old girl and not feel a little bit of understanding toward her. Is ticketing first time offenders a huge source of revenue for the city?

This brings me to another subject. When my daughter phoned me hysterically about the ticket, I explained to her about traffic court, how we would appear and the judge would reduce her fine for doing so. I was outraged that just the opposite was true. What is the point of showing up in traffic court? I could have gone to City Hall the very next day and paid the fine and not bothered to take her to court, but I thought it would be good for her to go and experience the seriousness of what she had done; be responsible. It took a lot of courage for her to stand up in front of approximately forty people and admit that she did something wrong, I don't know that could have done it at her age, I would have been so scared.

I am very unhappy with the traffic control in the city. I have lived here for one year, and as a real estate agent have sold or been involved in the sale of approximately 20 homes in the new subdivision, bringing a lot to the tax base in this little city. I have always told clients about what a great place it is to live, how safe it is, but I have decided to move after this incident. We need officers to keep our city safe, and traffic regulated, but also need them to be compassionate with our youth, and I did not see that demonstrated in this instance.

Thank You,
Mrs. Dainty

The court recognizes one's need to speak one's mind, and one's right to do so, both individually and on behalf of one's daughter. The letter is consistent with other letters where within the first paragraph there is an admission of guilt. Thus, one would wonder why the rest of the letter is necessary. But one must forge on to gain the full appreciation of the defense offered and understand the true sentiment that is expressed.

One of the common defenses in this type of letter is "I was emotionally upset by the entire experience." In this case, mom states that the daughter broke down in tears. While the court understands the shock of receiving one's first ticket, a speeding ticket is hardly worthy of tears. Mom then continues with the "my child is a good kid, therefore she is entitled to one free one—I knew I was speeding, but ought to get away with it one time" defense card. You know, the one get-out-of-jail-free card. Unfortunately, the legislature has not recognized that as a defense and therefore has not created a "one free speeding" exception.

Getting back to the point I began with in this vignette. The court is unable to determine from viewing a defendant what that person's mother has told them will happen. My ability to read people's minds is definitely limited. I am left with trying to understand some body language and what they verbally communicate. Absent communication from mother regarding what she had told her daughter, it is difficult for the court to take that into consideration. Had I known mom had told daughter if she appeared in court the judge would reduce her fine, I would have at least explained why the minimum fine was imposed.

Addressing a couple of mom's other points: her outrage is so great that she will move out of town? She has either led a very sheltered life or is disingenuous about her reason for changing her domicile, or, maybe she is not really going to move. What do you think?

At the end of the day, Ms. Dainty was caught with her hand in the cookie jar. The statutory minimum fine was imposed. Hopefully, it was a learning experience for her and perhaps for her mother. All things being equal, taking into consideration all points raised by Ms. Dainty's mom, I anticipate a restful night's sleep, a conscience free of guilt, and a sense of gratitude to

Ms. Dainty's mom for having spent the time to write the letter to brighten my day and contribute to the book.

THE YOUNG AND THE PREPARED

WHEN RECEIVING A TRAFFIC CITATION, individuals have several options. They can appear in court, which is by far the most common selection of the cited. Or, there are instructions on the back of the individual's copy of the citations that advise them that they can enter a plea in writing. A person can also submit a letter to the court explaining the circumstances.

The plea options are guilty, not guilty, or no contest. If either a guilty plea or no-contest plea is selected, the person is notified what fine the court imposed. If a not-guilty plea is entered, the matter will be set for a trial.

This case came before the court on two citations: one for failure to obey a traffic-control device and the other for driving while suspended. The court received a letter pleading not guilty to driving while suspended and guilty to failing to obey a traffic-control device, and requesting a trial. The individual, Mr. Heady, also indicated that he was a student at a state college in the northern part of the state. He asked if the trial could be set for the month of June. At the time, June was a few months off. The request was made because Mr. Heady would be on summer break at that time and would be home for the summer and in the area at that time. His trial was scheduled accordingly.

To understand the statement that Mr. Heady made a little later, I need to remind you of the chronology followed for the court docket. First, the court takes the matters for those individuals who are appearing in prison greens and law-enforcement-issued jewelry. Second, we take new appearances. Third, we take what we call our "pay or appear" patrons. These are those individuals, that mass of humanity, who have decided that they are simply not going to pay their fines and will outlast the court by appearing in court repeatedly, being rude or indifferent, and attempting to be very obnoxious to the court. Finally, at the end, we do trials. Trials are a very small percentage of the number of cases we hear.

On this particular afternoon, we had completed the docket all the way down to the trials. There were only two trials on the docket that day. The first was a not-guilty plea on a speeding ticket. That trial followed a very predictable pattern. The officer had clocked the individual with radar, which indicated that he was speeding. The individual admitted to speeding but denied going as fast as the officer alleged. The difference between the alleged speed and what the officer cited made no difference to the fine that would be imposed, so that case was dispensed of in a routine fashion.

That left Mr. Heady. He was a young man, eighteen or nineteen years of age. Dressed in a nice shirt and slacks, his hair cut, clean, with a very pleasant attitude. By his demeanor, I could tell that he was eager to have his say on his day in court.

The court calls the case. Mr. Heady bounds up to take his

place in front of the bench. The officer approaches, and the court begins.

"Officer, could you raise your hand to be sworn …"

Mr. Heady interrupts, "Your Honor, you do not need to have him testify. Everything he is going to tell you is the truth."

"Mr. Heady, I appreciate your candor. However, as a matter of procedure and protocol, I do need to hear the officer's testimony first."

"I am sorry, Your Honor, I was not trying to interfere. But … well … I will just wait. Thank you."

"Officer, let's swear you in and you can give me your *prima fascia* case. Do you solemnly swear the testimony you give will be the truth, the whole truth, and nothing but the truth?"

The officer responds, "Yes, Your Honor."

"Officer, we are proceeding on a not-guilty plea on the driving-while-suspended. We have, by written letter from Mr. Heady, a guilty plea for the failure to obey a traffic-control device. Therefore, I need to hear the *prima fascia* case regarding the driving-while-suspended only. You may go ahead."

"Well, Your Honor, I stopped Mr. Heady because he did not make a complete stop at a stop sign. When I pulled him over, I ran his license and it came back suspended. When I advised Mr. Heady that his license was suspended, he was shocked. He was very surprised. In fact, I wrote in my notes he said, and I quote, 'No way.' I went back and asked dispatch to verify again because he seemed genuinely surprised and convinced that he had a valid license. Dispatch confirmed that his driving license was suspended, so I issued a citation for driving while suspended."

"OK, Officer, thank you. Mr. Heady, do you have any questions to ask the officer in cross-examination?"

"No, Your Honor, I just want to tell you what happened."

"Very well, Mr. Heady, raise your right hand and be sworn. Do you solemnly swear that the testimony you give will be the truth, the whole truth, and nothing but the truth?"

"Yes, sir."

"Go ahead, sir."

And he began with a memorable quote, "Your Honor, I am not like the rest of these people in your courtroom today. I am a good person. I am a student up at the university, and I am trying to make something out of my life."

It is not possible for me to convey with written word the tone of this statement. It is not a statement made in arrogance. It is not a statement made to be derogatory of other people. It is a statement made to identify himself as a person with direction and purpose as compared to other individuals appearing before the court who were floundering in mediocrity and failure.

And he goes on, "Clear last summer, Your Honor, I had a job working for a farmer. Farm work is hard, but it was the only work I could find to make money to go to college. So, I worked a lot of hours. One day I was driving a farm truck delivering a load of hay. I got stopped for a broken taillight and was cited then because the truck did not have current registration. I turned the ticket over to the guy I was working for. He promised me he would take care of it. I wanted to be sure that it was taken care of, so a couple weeks later I asked him if he had taken care of it. He told me he had. Well, as it turns out, he did not take care of it. That court, which was not you, sent letters to the address that the Department of Motor Vehicles had for my address. However, I had moved, and the DMV had screwed up and did not change my address. I know, Your Honor, you probably hear that a lot. But, I have got my receipt here showing I sent in my change of address."

He produces a piece of paper, which is forwarded to the bench and which, in fact, confirms notice to the DMV of change of address.

"Thank you, Mr. Heady. It does appear the DMV failed to change your address as was requested by your notice."

"Yes, sir. So all those letters from the DMV and from the court were going to an address where I was not getting them. After I did not respond to the letters, the court suspended my license. Once again, the DMV sent me a letter to the wrong address. I have a copy of the letter here that I got from the DMV a couple of months ago."

Once again, the document is forwarded to the court; it is a copy of the suspension notice going to the wrong address.

"So, I did not know I was suspended. I also did not know my boss had not taken care of the ticket. Since then, I have done everything I can to take care of the matter. To get this taken care of, I went back to the DMV to give them a new change of address."

Once again, a document with a new change of address is forwarded to the bench. This time, receipt of the change has been acknowledged by the department of motor vehicles.

He continues, "I sent a letter to the guy I worked for telling him that he needed to get that ticket taken care of and that he was going to have to pay for all my expense in taking care of this mess. Here is a copy of the letter. I then went to the other court and explained to them what happened. That judge dismissed that ticket when I showed him what had happened. Here is a copy of the dismissal from that court. My old boss still has not been willing to take care of things like I think he should. So, I filed a claim in small claims court to have him pay me for what I have lost in expenses, having to clear all this up and having to be here. And here is a copy of the small-claims-court document."

His documents are forwarded up. Each and every document confirms what Mr. Heady is saying.

He continues, "I am not trying to say anything bad about other people, but I am a good person. I am going to school. I am trying to do the things I am supposed to do. I have a job this summer working at the bank, and I will be going back to college in the fall. I may have been driving while I was suspended, but I did not know I was, and I do not think I did anything wrong, so I should not be guilty of the driving-while-suspended. Now, on that running the stop sign, yeah, I plead guilty to that, because I am not sure whether I did or did not stop. I usually stop at stop signs. If you will look at my driving record, I have never had a traffic ticket of any kind. The officer says I did not do a complete stop and I think I did, but I really do not know, so I just plead guilty because I do not know for sure. I do not think I am guilty of driving while suspended. I do not know what words you want to use, but I do not think I should be found guilty for it."

"Mr. Heady, I think the term you are looking for is you think the citation should be dismissed. Officer, is there any other evidence you would like the court to consider."

The officer responds, "Well, Your Honor, depending on

what you do with driving while suspended, I would like to be heard on the failure to obey the traffic-control device."

"Very well. Mr. Heady, at this time, based on the evidence before me, I will dismiss the driving-while-suspended citation. Though I think you technically were guilty because you in fact were suspended, I believe the extenuating circumstances clearly indicated that you did not know you were. Furthermore, I find that you took every reasonable effort to deal with your other citation. You are one of the few people I know that has actually filed a change-of-address form with the DMV when they were supposed to. Officer, you asked to be heard on the failure to obey traffic-control device."

The officer responds, "Yes, Your Honor. Your Honor, when I pulled Mr. Heady over, he was in fact very surprised about the driving-while-suspended. He was polite and cordial throughout the entire time. I initially expected only to give him a warning about running the stop sign. However, when he was suspended, I wrote him up for both citations. Based on that, Your Honor, and in the interest of justice, I would ask the court to dismiss the failure to obey the traffic-control device."

"Motion to dismiss is granted. Mr. Heady, thank you for the cordial and professional way in which you conducted yourself here today. Good luck in school. Both of your citations will be dismissed."

He gathered his papers and placed them back neatly into the folder in which he had brought them. He shook hands with the officers, thanked the court, and went back to work at the bank.

Somewhere out there is a mother who should be glowing

with pride. My wish would be that all humanity could soar so gracefully over the bumps in life.

Out of Sight ...
Dang ... Still a Problem

IN ONE OF THE JURISDICTIONS in which I serve, finding a suitable space for a courtroom has been a continuing and ongoing challenge. We started out meeting in the council chambers at City Hall. When the city staff needed additional office space, a row of offices was built along the back wall of the council chamber. That reduced the size of the room and, while it accommodated the few people who had any interest in city council, the remaining space did not accommodate the larger and largely involuntary congregation that attended court.

So, arrangements were made for the court to meet at the Grange Hall, a large, rectangular room, stark and empty. A table was set up at one end of the room. Behind the table, the court and clerks would sit. The audience sat in folding chairs aligned in rows. To the audience's back was the door through which they entered and then left. To the court's back was a kitchen. However, the absence of heat in the winter led to allegations of cruel and unusual punishment by the court and staff. So, more suitable and habitable facilities were sought.

Our next domicile was the community playhouse. The community playhouse was once again a large rectangular room with an elevated stage area one step up from floor level. The seating was traditional: old-fashioned, curved-back wooden tilt-up seats, theater seating bolted to the floor in rows of approximately twelve to fifteen. There were a dozen or so rows. For several months one summer, the backdrop on the stage was arranged for a play that was being performed at the playhouse. Each evening before court began, the clerks would produce a large, stained drop cloth to cover a six-foot painting on black velvet of a nude female lying on a couch. It was part of the set for the play.

Eventually, the playhouse needed additional office space and, once again, the court was looking for a new home. We briefly went back into the city council chambers, which were still too small, for a few months and then were accepted into our current home, the community center.

There was a different atmosphere at each location, as well as experiences due to the functionality or non-functionality of aspects of the facility. For example, when court appeared in the city council chambers, the council bench actually sat at floor level. To give the council an appearance of elevated status, the council table, which doubled for the bench, was approximately four and a half feet high. The council members and the mayor sat on stools so that while sitting they could peer out from over the bench. I found this particularly workable because I could stand behind the bench or sit on the stool that was provided, depending on the general condition of my backside or feet. While court was in session, I sat or stood behind the corner of the L-shaped counter. This allowed defendants to walk up to the center of the opposite side of the bench and stand approximately two feet away from me. This was far too intimate for the judicial/defendant relationship. This situation was remedied by placing a small table about four feet out from the bench, which gave the court some distance from the bad breath and body odor of the defendants, and also was out of arm's reach so as not to encourage errant punches or attacks. When the crowd overwhelmed the room, we would have a number of people standing in a hallway and then outside. Thus, as the court called a name, a spontaneous relay was developed whereby a name would be repeated, then repeated, and then repeated. An echo sort of effect. For example, after I called a name, such as Joe Smith, in the back of the courtroom, one of the audience would yell "Joe Smith" down the hallway, which would be followed by one more relay to someone standing in the doorway yelling "Joe Smith" to the crowd outside. The reverse relay would then return, hence the echo effect, with either "not here, not here, not here," or "he's coming, he's coming, he's coming." While this encouraged group and crowd involvement, it was not the most efficient way to run court.

At the Grange Hall, the challenges were the lighting and heating during the winter. The lighting was very poor in that big, open room, and on two occasions, the temperature in the courtroom hovered in the mid-thirties due to failure of what pretended to be a heating unit. But the court proceeded.

I shared all of that with you so that as I describe this next event, you will appreciate the setting in which it occurred. This next episode happened while court was located in the community playhouse. Remember, the seating was bolted to the floor in long rows.

On this particular evening, I was running just a little later than normal. I arrived at courthouse about ten minutes before court was due to start. As I was walking up the steps through the crowd of people who had assembled outside, the doors to the playhouse suddenly burst open and out came three officers, one clearing the way, the other two on either side of a handcuffed, disheveled individual being partially carried and partially dragged. As the entourage exited, they went down the stairs out to a police car. I watched long to enough to see two officers unceremoniously stuff the man into the back seat of the police car. Upon entering the courtroom, I saw yet another man holding a wad of wet paper towels to his face, trying to stop the bleeding of a small facial wound. There was blood on his shirt, his eyes were wide, and he was talking frantically in a very high-pitched, loud voice.

Needless to say, this is not the ordinary scene that greets me when I arrive at court. Working my way through the courtroom, I noticed the sheet rock on one wall was broken and caved in. Working my way through the melee, I found my clerks and inquired as to what had occurred. A clerk advised me that there had been a, shall we say, fracas. The man out in the police car in handcuffs and the man whose face was bleeding were neighbors. Police-car boy was to have appeared that night on a citation for, are you ready for this, disposing of trash in his backyard by a method not allowed by the city ordinance.

It seems as though police-car boy, hereinafter referred to as Mr. Calm, had the use of a backhoe one afternoon. He decided that, rather than pay the fees for trash disposal either for the trash collection service or through fees at the local landfill, he would create his own landfill. In his backyard, with the backhoe, he dug a substantial hole. His plan was to fill the hole with garbage over the course of several years and, when it had reached near-surface level, he would restore the earth back on top of it, thus saving himself the expense of disposal of his trash.

I do not want to understate the size of this hole. Later, I saw a photograph of the garbage hole Mr. Calm had dug. One of the identifiable items in the bottom of hole was a damaged and unusable fourteen-foot aluminum boat.

The man with his face bleeding was Mr. Calm's neighbor, Mr. Nasal. It seems that Mr. Nasal and Mr. Calm were not on the city water system. They each had their own private wells. Both wells were sixty to eighty feet deep. Mr. Nasal was irate over the garbage dump for several reasons including smell, flies, rodents, and vermin. But mostly, his concern was the threat of contamination of his water source. A valid concern.

The depth of the hole dug by Mr. Calm was such that it reduced the distance between the water level in Mr. Nasal's well and the surface by about ten to twelve feet. Mr. Nasal was rightfully very concerned about contamination of his water. Mr. Calm, on the other hand, was not as concerned about the water supply or his or his family's overall health. Apparently, he had not considered the possibility of seepage.

Mr. Nasal and Mr. Calm had had an ongoing feud for several years. While at this point in time I was unaware of the all the reasons for the conflict, future events would shed light, ,insight and greater understanding on this neighborly clash.

Not only were there trash-disposal issues, but it seems that the Calms had a dog who liked to chase and growl at children and adults and, as it later turned out, police officers. So, put an indifferent, bad neighbor next to a high-pitched, shrill-voiced, nasal whiner and you have your basic volatile situation.

It is not uncommon for individuals who lodge complaints that result in citations to appear in court to find out the disposition of "their" matter. On this particular evening, Mr. Calm and his wife had come to court for Mr. Calm's first appearance on the citation. Mr. Nasal, his wife, his neighbor, and two of his kids had come to observe. Mr. Calm and his wife had been sitting in about the second row of chairs in the courtroom, waiting for court to start. Mr. Nasal and his entourage entered the courtroom and sat about two rows behind Mr. Calm. Whereupon, Mr. Nasal, in his nasal, whiny, high-pitched way, began his endless diatribe of comments about the universe in general and Mr. Calm in particular.

Mr. Calm, by outward appearances, would appear to be a mild-mannered individual. Something around five feet four to five feet five inches, medium build, light brown hair, round, cherubic sort of face. When he spoke, he spoke softly. And when he moved, he moved rather slowly and lethargically. However, on this particular occasion, Mr. Calm deviated from his normal practice. When his patience had been exhausted, he sprang to his feet, turned around, and, using his seat for a single step, launched himself across the two or three rows of fixed chairs that separated him and Mr. Nasal and dove headfirst into Mr. Nasal. The two men then wrestled among the chairs while the police officers attempted to separate them, dragging them from the seating area out into an aisle. The police officers were struggling to gain control of the situation when Mr. Calm shoved one police officer back into the wall, where he crashed partially through the wall, damaging the sheet rock. In the free-for-all, Mr. Nasal's face became scratched and began bleeding. When order was finally restored to the courtroom, Mr. Calm was handcuffed, removed from the court, and taken out into the police car. Thereafter, he was lodged in the county jail on an assault charge.

Within minutes of Mr. Calm's removal from the courtroom, the docket had been reviewed, the clerks were seated behind the bench, the bailiff was present, and court began.

Mr. Calm appeared in circuit court on the felony assault charge. The judge in that court, following the protocol for violent assaults, ordered Mr. Calm to stay away from Mr. Nasal and the city court. This created a mild dilemma because Mr. Calm still needed to appear on his citation. The court clerk spoke to the county court clerk—essentially, my people spoke to that judge's people—and worked it out so that Mr. Calm could appear at the next court date. However, he had to arrive twenty minutes before court was due to start and find a city police officer and stay right by that police officer's side during the entire time he was in court. Thus, two weeks later, Mr. Calm appeared in court accompanied by his uniformed, badge-wearing, gun-carrying chaperone. There he stood, quiet, soft eyes, mild-mannered, very docile, and entered a not-guilty plea for the unlawful disposal of trash.

Trial was scheduled for two weeks later. Two weeks went by. Both Mr. Calm and Mr. Nasal brought their entire entourages to this long-awaited event. Neighbors, friends, relatives, curious onlookers, pretty much everything short of pets. When the case was called, Mr. Calm, with his chaperone in tow, took his place in front of the bench. The officer who had written the citation was sworn in, and testimony went something like this:

"I was called to the address located on Blank Street where Mr. Nasal resides. I have been to that address and to the neighboring address on many occasions to resolve disputes between these two neighbors. Mr. Calm and Mr. Nasal and their families have a long, ongoing fight. However, on this occasion, Mr. Nasal was complaining that Mr. Calm had created a garbage dump in his backyard. I accompanied Mr. Nasal to his backyard where I could see over the fence and there was indeed a big hole in Mr. Calm's backyard. I could not see the bottom of the hole from Mr. Nasal's backyard so I went next door, where I contacted Mr. Calm. I asked if I could inspect Mr. Calm's backyard. He consented and accompanied me to the backyard. In the backyard, there was a large hole that had been dug by a backhoe. There was a pile of dirt in the back of the yard and this large hole. In the large hole, there was a lot of garbage that had been dumped in the hole. The hole was big enough that there was a twelve- to fourteen-foot aluminum boat down in the hole. There were grass and tree clippings and what appeared to be garbage from their house down in the hole. I advised Mr. Calm that he could not have a garbage dump or a landfill in his backyard. I then cited Mr. Calm for violation of the city ordinance."

At this point, Mr. Nasal and his entourage in the back of the courtroom begin talking quite loudly. Mr. Nasal directs his comments at the court, attempting to advise the court of everything else that might have been in the hole. I bring the court back to order, advising Mr. Nasal and his gaggle that they will have to remain silent while in the courtroom. The court will not tolerate interruptions, and they will be removed from the courtroom if they do not comply.

The court to Mr. Calm: "Mr. Calm, would you like to question the officer regarding his testimony? This would be your opportunity to cross-examine this witness."

"No, Your Honor, I would just like to explain what happened. I would like to explain what I was doing."

"Very well, Mr. Calm, raise your right hand and be sworn."

Whereupon, Mr. Calm is sworn in and begins, "Your Honor, we had rented a backhoe for a job I was working on, and I brought it home one evening to do a little bit of work at my house. The garbage fees and landfill fees have really gone up a lot. So, I just thought I would dig a hole where I could throw away the stuff we did not want to use to save on our dump fees. I did not know it was a violation of the city ordinance."

"Mr. Calm, as you are now aware that it is a violation of the city ordinance, can the court assume that you will take care of this matter?"

"Well, Your Honor, I am gonna have to see how I could take care of that."

"Mr. Calm, is there any other evidence you would like me to consider?"

"No, sir."

"Very well. The court will find you guilty on the citation as charged. I will order that the disposal site be cleaned up and taken care of within thirty days of today. When you have it taken care of, you are to notify the chief of police, who will have an officer inspect your backyard and make sure that it is done. Assuming you take care of things the way you should, that will resolve that aspect and the court will also impose the minimum fine allowed by that ordinance. And that will be all for tonight. Mr. Nasal, I will need to have you and everybody with you stay seated in the courtroom for a few minutes. Officer, if you can escort Mr. Calm and all of his guests to the back door, we will give them a few minute head start so that we do not have another free-for-all in the parking lot. Mr. Calm, you and all those with you are ordered to leave the building and the parking lot immediately. Does everybody understand that?"

"Yes," echoes throughout the courtroom, whereupon Mr. Calm and his troupe leave. We handle one more trial and in about five minutes dismiss Mr. Nasal and his fan club.

At this point, you would think this case is over, wouldn't you? I did. But no, we would be wrong. Two weeks go by. Next court date, among my pre-court agenda items, is an inquiry as to whether Mr. Calm has taken care of his problem. The chief of police advises me that he personally had been to the backyard and saw where the hole had been filled with dirt. Mr. Calm advised him that the matter was taken care of. We go on into court. I notice Mr. Nasal's presence in the court. When we are finished with the docket, Mr. Nasal remains. Though in my heart of hearts I knew I would like to avoid the next phase of this encounter, such was not to be the case.

"Mr. Nasal, I see you are in court again this evening. Is it that you have just grown to like us, or do you have a matter for the court?"

Mr. Nasal rises, and in his nasal, high-pitched, auctioneer-paced speech pattern, which can best be described as diarrhea-of-the-mouth, begins his comments as he approaches the bench. I will not belabor the details of everything that he says and the complaints he has and derogatory comments regarding Mr. Calm. The gist of his comment is generally that Mr. Calm did not clean up the garbage dump that was in the bottom of the hole. He simply buried it. Mr. Nasal is advised that the matter will be investigated. He is invited to leave.

The police were dispatched to investigate the matter. As it turns out, Mr. Nasal was once again, although irritating, accurate. Mr. Calm thought he could resolve his issue by simply covering up what he had already deposited in the bottom of the hole. The chief of police advised him that the dirt would have to be excavated and all the trash removed. Mr. Calm thereafter complied and compliance was confirmed by the chief of police.

A job worth doing is worth doing twice. Or at least it was for Mr. Calm.

Not Every Dog Has Its Day, but Every Dog Owner Does

THE CITATION AT ISSUE IN this case is generally referred to as "dog at large." The city ordinance describes the prohibited act as "allowing a dog to run at large." Boiled down to the basic, simplest explanation, this means that if you own a dog, it has got to be in your yard, or under your care and control if the dog is outside of your yard. Not complex stuff here, right?

To increase the likelihood that the dog will stay in their yard, most people install an adequate fence. The care or control of the dog outside of the yard is generally managed with a leash. Neither of these concepts is complex either. However, you would be surprised at the difficulties some people have grasping these simple rules.

Remember Mr. Calm, who had the trash dumped in his backyard? Well, Mr. and Mrs. Calm also had a dog. Now, if you were the Calms, what kind of dog do you think you would have? You are right. A pit bull-Rottweiler cross; a mean-looking dog, of course. Go ahead, ponder this question for a moment: what do you think the odds are that the Calms have an adequate fence around their yard or maintains the dog in their care, custody, and control at all times? You've got it—not a chance.

As court begins this particular evening, it is a light docket. Not many people in the courtroom. As I enter the court with the traditional ceremony of everybody rising when I enter, I note that Mr. Calm is in the audience with his wife and a couple of children. I immediately scan the audience for his neighbor to see if we have another neighborly conflict going. No neighbor present. Good sign. We press ahead with the docket. About the fourth or fifth ticket into the first-appearance docket, there is Mr. Calm appearing on a citation for dog at large. Up to this point, I was unaware that Mr. Calm owned a dog. A garbage dump in his backyard, yes, but not a dog. Court calls his name.

"Mr. Calm."

He approaches. He moves through the courtroom with the look of a man familiar with his surroundings. Comfortable in the forum. Acts almost pleased to be there.

"Mr. Calm, you are appearing on a citation for dog at large. How do you plead?"

"Your Honor, I plead not guilty."

"Very well, the matter will be set for trial two weeks from tonight. Mr. Calm, you need to return at that time and bring any evidence or witnesses you would like me to consider. The court will provide you with a notice. Once you have signed the notice and check in with the officer at the back, you will be free to leave. Thank you for appearing."

Mr. Calm picks up his paperwork, checks in at the back.

Seasoned, experienced defendants are always more efficient than rookies.

Two weeks go by. It is the night set for trial. As we start the trial, I notice several people still in the courtroom. Once again, I am curious as to how they are going to participate in this process.

The case is called. Two police officers approach the bench along with Mr. Calm. The trial goes something like this.

"This is the time and place set for trial in the matter of the city versus Mr. Calm. We are proceeding on a not-guilty plea on a citation for a dog at large. Officers, is the city ready to proceed?"

"Yes, Your Honor, we are ready."

"Mr. Calm, are you ready to proceed?"

"Yes, Your Honor, I am ready."

"Officer, if you will raise your right hand and be sworn," whereupon the officer raises his right hand and is sworn. "Officer, go ahead with your case." And the officer begins:

"On the blankety-blank day of blankety-blank month, at about 6:00 PM, I was on duty in the city dressed as I am here today in full uniform, badge prominently displayed. I was on patrol with the officer standing next to me, in the neighborhood and on the street where Mr. Calm lives. As we were entering that street, we saw a large dog chasing kids and an adult, who are obviously afraid of the dog. When we reached the area where the dog was, the officer who was with me and I got out of the car to assist in the matter. At that time, the dog charged directly at me and attempted to bite me. I was able to avoid being bitten by moving out of the dog's way and pushing him away with my baton. While all this was going on,

Mrs. Calm and her children were in their front yard watching the dog chase people. After the dog came at me, Mrs. Calm and one of the children came out and grabbed the dog and took it back into their yard. We have had many calls on this dog. Mr. Calm does not seem to be able to control his dog. After several attempts to try to encourage Mr. Calm to control the dog, we issued the citation for him to come to court."

"Thank you. Mr. Calm, do you have any questions you would like to ask the officer, as in cross-examination of anything the officer has said?"

"No, sir, I just want to tell you what happened."

"Very well, raise your right hand and be sworn," whereupon Mr. Calm is placed under oath.

"Well, I was not even there when all this happened. There may have been a time or two when the dog was out, but we try to control the dog. He is a big dog, but he is really good with the kids and he never has hurt anybody. If you will just be nice to him, the dog is very nice. Our kids play with it all the time. Anyway, my wife told me that she and the kids were right in the front yard with the dog all the time and it was only out of our yard for just a little minute or so."

"OK, is there anything else you'd like to tell me?"

"Yes, Your Honor, there is one other thing. I do not think I should have got the ticket because it is not my dog."

"Really? Whose dog is it?"

"It is my wife's dog."

"Officer, would you like to respond to that last statement?"

"Well, Your Honor, the day we issued the citation, Mrs. Calm told us that it was her husband's dog. This is the first time we have heard that it is not his dog. Like I said, we have been to the house several times and we have always been told that the dog belonged to Mr. Calm. Can I ask the court a question, Your Honor?"

"Go ahead."

"If I were to move to dismiss this citation, could I reissue the citation to Mrs. Calm?"

"The court is not aware of any legal restriction to what you are proposing."

"Very well. If I might have a moment, Your Honor."

Whereupon, the officer leaves the room and comes back with his notebook. From the notebook, he takes out a fresh citation which he fills out for Mrs. Calm. He then walks to the back of the courtroom, hands the citation to her, comes back to the front of the courtroom, and states:

"Your Honor, I move to dismiss the citation against Mr. Calm, if this is not his dog."

"Very well, the citation will be dismissed. Mr. Calm, you are free to go. Mrs. Calm, would you please approach the bench? Mrs. Calm, you have just been served a citation for a dog at large. Would you like to address the matter right now, or would you like to wait for a later court date?"

Mrs. Calm responds, "I want to wait till a different court date."

"OK. However, you will be required to at least enter a plea here tonight. How do you plead?"

"Not guilty."

"Very well, trial will be set two weeks from tonight. You need to return at that time, bringing any and all evidence or witnesses you would like the court to consider."

Two weeks go by. Court wanders through the docket, the

failures to appear, the pay-or-appears, the appearances from jail. We finally get to the trials. The court notes that the same basic group of people is still in the courtroom as was there before. I will not bore you with the recitation of how the first part of the trial goes. Suffice it to say, the officer repeats the testimony, directing the comments at Mrs. Calm, who now stands in front of the bench. When the officer is finished with his testimony, she is offered a chance for cross-examination, which she declines. Thereafter, she is sworn in and testifies as follows.

"Well, Your Honor, I was out there the entire time. I saw the whole thing. Like my husband told you the other night, the dog is just real playful. It never has hurt anybody. Our kids play with it all the time. I heard the officer say that the dog has been out and been a problem a lot. If the dog had been such a big problem, then somebody should have told us. No one has ever complained about the dog before this time. So, I think this case should be dismissed."

"Officer, would you like to respond to the testimony offered by Mrs. Calm?"

"Yes, Your Honor, we would. We would like to call a witness."

"Very well, call your next witness."

"The city will now call the county animal control officer who is present in the court."

Whereupon, the uniformed animal control officer approaches and is sworn in.

"Sir, were you there the day the citation was issued?"

"I got there a little later after the citation already had been issued, but I have been there many times before. I have been to the Calms' residence on fourteen different occasions to talk to them about their dog and to deal with complaints with their dog."

Mrs. Calm interrupts, "You have not been to our house fourteen times."

The court: "Ma'am, you need to wait your turn. You will need to be quiet while this witness testifies. You will be given a chance to cross-examine the witness and respond to anything he said."

Back to the animal control officer: "Ma'am, I have a list right here of every time I have been to your house. Would you like to hear it?"

Mrs. Calm says, "No, that will not be necessary."

The court: "Yes, Officer, I would like to hear that list."

The officer then reads through his notes and identifies dates, times, and incidents involving numerous neighbors. The same dog with the same type of conduct. When he finishes with his list, the animal control officer states, "Your Honor, this dog has been a problem for a long time. I am glad that finally they have been issued a citation, and maybe we can get the Calms to control their dog."

Throughout the testimony of the animal control officer, Mrs. Calm glares, stares, grits her teeth and, a time or two, I think I see a snarl, a form of expression she seems have picked up from her dog.

The court: "Thank you, Officer. Mrs. Calm, do you have any questions for this witness?"

"No!" she states emphatically.

"Officer, you are excused. Does the city have any other witnesses?"

"There are a lot of other neighbors here, but they were not here on this citation. So, no, not at this time."

"Mrs. Calm, please remember that you are still under oath. Do you have anything else you would like to say?"

"Yes, I would!"

"Mrs. Calm, please go ahead."

"I was there that day. I saw the whole thing. But that was not my dog."

There it was. The bombshell was dropped again. Looks of shock and amazement on the faces of all the officers and clerks, and probably on mine. She continues, "That is right. That was not my dog. It looks a lot like my dog but it is not. And I have a witness to prove it. Can I have my witness testify?"

"Certainly."

"Mr. Witness is here, sitting back there." She points to the back of the courtroom.

"Mr. Witness, please come forward and be sworn in."

Mr. Witness comes forward and is sworn in and begins.

"Your Honor, I need to make sure that I have the right date. Can you tell me what day the citation was written on?"

"Certainly, sir. The citation was issued on blankety-blank date at about blankety-blank time."

"I live out of town about eight miles. On that date, on that afternoon, Mr. Calm was at my house, and he had his dog with him. I do not know which dog they are talking about here, but Mr. Calm brings his dog out to my house all the time. His dog plays with my dog and they have a great time. On that particular day, I do remember Mr. Calm being at my house with his dog."

The court, "Are you certain it was that date?"

"Yes, Your Honor, I am pretty sure."

"Very well. Officer (the animal control officer), how do you know it was Mrs. Calm's dog the day the citation was issued?"

The animal control officer responds, "Your Honor, I am very familiar with the dog. I have been to Mr. and Mrs. Calm's house on several occasions. It is the only dog that looks like that. I would recognize the dog anywhere."

The officer responds, "Your Honor, we are all very familiar with this dog. That was their dog present that day."

"Very well, thank you. Mrs. Calm, is there any other evidence you would like to present?"

"No, Your Honor, there is not."

"Very well, I am prepared to rule on this case. Mrs. Calm, I find you guilty of violation of the dog-at-large ordinance. It appears that the animal control officer, the city, and your neighbors have all been very patient waiting for you to understand the importance of controlling your dog. I will impose the minimum fine at this time since this is your first offense in front of the court. However, be advised that the maximum fine is substantial and if you do not manage your dog, I will impose the maximum fine on you each and every time you appear on a dog-at-large citation in the future. Do you understand that?"

"Yes, Your Honor."

"Are you able to pay the fine tonight or do you need to make payments?"

"Well, Your Honor, since this was not my dog, I am not going to pay this fine." True righteous indignation billowing out of a not-so-composed Mrs. Calm.

"Very well, ma'am. You need to appear twice a month in court until such a time as you agree to a payment schedule or pay the fine. If you fail to appear in court, I will issue a warrant for your arrest. Do you understand that?"

"You better get used to seeing me a lot, because I am going to be here. It's not fair. It's not right, and I am not going to pay this ticket."

"Your choice. That will be all tonight. Your next appearance is two weeks from tonight unless you want to talk about a payment schedule. You apparently do not; therefore I will see you two weeks from tonight unless you pay the citation in full."

She turns abruptly, elevates her nose in the air, assumes an air of disdain, and prisses out of the courtroom.

For the next several months, Mrs. Calm appears at every court session. She waits her turn and then with the same indignant attitude, approaches the bench, indicates that she is still not going to pay the fine, and leaves. Over this time, she develops a friendship with another regular. The friendship is with an individual who by reputation practices the world's oldest profession. I will refer to her as Ms. Hooks. Mrs. Calm and Ms. Hooks sit together during court and visit. They wait till each other has appeared and then leave together. What a beautiful thing; a friendship like this warms the cockles of your heart.

As the weeks go on, Mrs. Calm and Ms. Hooks introduce a new practice, more of a malicious-compliance approach. They are not there when court begins. They start appearing later in the court session after their names have already been called. This creates an inconvenience for the court, as their files have to be retrieved from those that have already been set aside and completed. Finally, on one evening, both Mrs. Calm and Ms. Hooks are present after being late. The conversation goes something like this:

"Mrs. Calm, and Ms Hooks, you were ordered by the court to be here at 7:00 PM. That means that you have to be here at 7:00 PM. If you are not here at 7:00 PM, I will impose an appropriate penalty to encourage you to be here on time."

Mrs. Calm: "But we do not have to be here till our name is called."

"No, Mrs. Calm, you were ordered to be here at a specific time and you need to be here at that time."

"If you are going to make us come at seven o'clock, then you ought to call us at seven o'clock."

"Now, there is a point on which reasonable minds might differ. However, in this particular setting, your opinion is of little value. Let me make this very clear to you, to both of you. You are ordered to appear at seven o'clock, two weeks from tonight. If you do not appear as scheduled, I will issue a warrant for failure to appear. Do both of you understand that?"

They respond with yes, turn on their heels, and head for the door. Now, Mrs. Calm is a tall, slender woman with large, pronounced facial features, whereas Ms. Hooks is somewhat shorter and more amply endowed from the neck down. Sort of a "Mutt and Jeff" combination. The thinking and reasoning that went into their approach is hard to understand. They are appearing in a forum over which they have no control. They are not familiar with options, possibilities, processes, or remedies. In a scenario where one might try to encourage favor, or at least not antagonize, they seem to be intentionally attempting to invoke the frustration or irritation of the court.

Now, I am not the sharpest knife in the drawer, but my cutting edge is significantly sharper than Mrs. Calm's and Ms. Hooks's. As they depart, I turn to the court clerk and request that warrants for failure to appear be prepared for both Mrs. Calm and Ms. Hooks and that the dates be left blank on the warrants. The warrants should be available at the opening of court two weeks from that night.

Two weeks go by. Next court date. As I approach the courtroom that evening, I notice outside the court, Mrs. Calm and Ms. Hooks are present. Although they see me approaching, they turn and pretend they do not observe that I have arrived. I go to the courthouse. We take care of a few matters before court starts, and at seven o'clock sharp, court is called into session. We enter and court begins. As I enter the courtroom, I look around the courtroom, and Mrs. Calm and Ms. Hooks are not present. So, I call their names first.

"Mrs. Calm, are you present?" There is no response. Out loud so all the court can hear, I then state, "Very well, Mrs. Calm is not in court as ordered. I am hereby signing the warrant that has been prepared for Mrs. Calm for failure to appear as scheduled."

"Ms. Hooks, are you present?" Once again, no response. Once again, out loud, "Very well, if Ms. Hooks is not present in the courtroom, I am now signing a warrant for her arrest for failure to appear as scheduled."

Having accomplished that task, we move on with court.

First appearances are called and handled. The failures to appear on first appearances are then worked through the docket. Finally, we get to the pay-or-appears. We are about to complete the pay-or-appears when Mrs. Calm and Ms. Hooks sashay into the courtroom. Both women intentionally make direct eye contact with me and then sit in the back row. We finish the docket of pay-or-appears and move forward to handle three trials. When the last trial is complete, the only people left in the courtroom are Mrs. Calm, Ms. Hooks, the officers, the clerks, and me.

"Mrs. Calm and Ms. Hooks, could you please approach the bench? You were not here at seven o'clock as ordered to be. Therefore, I have signed warrants for your arrest. Officers, take them into custody."

Shock and disbelief, astonishment, surprise: I am searching for the right word to describe the looks on their faces as the officers handcuff them.

"You are to be lodged in the county jail. In all likelihood, you will be out tomorrow morning. You can always post bail. Bail is set at ten times the amount of your outstanding fines; therefore, if you post the 10 percent when you get to the County Jail, you will be released immediately. You are now ordered to appear two weeks from tonight at 7:00 PM, unless you have paid your citations in full. That is 7:00 PM; that is right after 6:59 PM and just before 7:01 PM. When I come into court at 7:00 PM, I expect to see you here unless you have paid your fines in full. If you are not here at 7:00 PM, I will issue new warrants for your arrest, and you will keep going through this little exercise in futility until you comply with the court's order. Are we very clear on this?"

Neither person says a word. Both nod in the affirmative.

The officers then remove them from the courtroom and off they go to the county jail.

I turn to the clerk and request that two more warrants be prepared, the dates to be left blank in anticipation of what might happen two weeks from that night.

Two weeks go by.

As I arrive at court on this evening, once again I see Mrs. Calm and Ms. Hooks standing outside the courtroom. This time I got dirty glares from them as I walked around to the side entrance to go into the courtroom. Once again, I took care of some preliminary pre-court matters and was prepared to start court at 7:00 PM sharp.

As court is called into session and we enter the room, once again I scan the audience for Mrs. Calm and Ms. Hooks. They are not present. I call their names first. Same sort of dialogue as before, and I execute the warrants immediately after their failure to appear. We start into the first-appearance docket.

About five minutes after 7:00 PM, the back door opens and in comes Mrs. Calm and Ms. Hooks. Same air of disdain, flaunting their late arrival at the court. On through the docket we go. When we get to the pay-or-appears, I deviate from my normal practice of following the alphabetical sequence of the docket.

"Mrs. Calm and Ms. Hooks, could you approach the bench?" They rise and arrive at the bench. "Once again, ladies, you did not appear as ordered. At seven o'clock when court began, your names were called. You were not present. Officers, take them back into custody and lodge them back in the county jail."

Ms. Hooks speaks up with a look of surprise and says, "You are not going to do this again, are you?"

"Yes, ma'am, I most certainly am. And I will continue to do it until you comply with the orders you are given from this court."

Mrs. Calm contributes her two bits: "This just is not fair."

"Mrs. Calm, quite frankly, the court is indifferent as to your opinion as to what is fair or not. Your lack of respect to this court has been duly noted. While I am totally indifferent as to your feelings or opinions of me, I will not tolerate disrespect for this institution. I will continue to lodge either or both of you until you comply with court orders. Please remember that you can post bail yet once again to avoid the experience of a night in jail."

At that point, the first chink in the armor is observed. Mrs. Calm attempts to blink back tears. Her countenance changes. While it would be an overstatement to say that she has had a change of heart, at a minimum there was a recognition that she is engaged in a battle in which she cannot win. The proverbial lightbulb is beginning to come on.

Ms. Hooks has a different approach. She asks to speak to an individual sitting in the back of the courtroom. After a brief conversation, she is placed in a police car with Mrs. Calm, transported, and lodged in the county jail.

Once again, I request new warrants are to be prepared in anticipation of the events coming up at the next court two weeks hence.

Two weeks go by.

Once again, I arrive at court. I see neither Mrs. Calm nor Ms. Hooks outside the court. Once inside, I am advised that Ms.

Hooks posted bail and was not lodged. Mrs. Calm had been unable to post bail and spent another night in jail. However, as court begins that night, Mrs. Calm is present in the court at 7:00 PM sharp. Sometime before the next appearance, her fine is paid in full.

Sometimes it just takes some folks a little longer to learn than it does other folks. Before one engages in battle, one must measure one's opponent and ensure that there is at least some possibility of success. Absent the possibility of success, one may well consider a different course of action. In the realm of the court, this institution is both the immovable object and the unstoppable force. This institution and the court will survive Ms. Hooks and Mrs. Calm—and me. Maintaining respect for the institution is paramount for the institution to function effectively. Not only did Mrs. Calm and Ms. Hooks learn a lesson, but all the regular court groupies observed the process and became much more diligent in their compliance for a while. Happy endings are always good.

MISTER MINI-NOT-
SO-TOUGH GUY

FROM TIME TO TIME, YOUNG, junior, wannabe bad guys make an appearance in court. The typical reasons for these diminutive deviants are either failure to wear a bike helmet or curfew violation. The officers typically do not write these citations unless they have an extensive history with the kids and talking and/or threatening do not seem to be working. As for the bike helmets, the police department keeps a supply on hand which they will give, without charge, to any young person who claims not to have one. So, after several attempts to encourage compliance, the officer will take that step of issuing a citation. And into court they come.

The age of these malefactors is usually fourteen down to nine or ten. With a child this age, you would think that they would be accompanied by a parental unit of some sort. Some are, and sadly, some are not. Being nine to fourteen, they do not have jobs and therefore have no real way to pay a fine. This generally results in either scenario one: good parents with bad kids are already struggling and a fine just adds to their challenges; or scenario two: crummy parents who are usually indifferent and will not pay, which results in a family experience of mocking the court. This was a real dilemma for me when I first started at the court.

After a few experiences with these juveniles, we came up with what we dubbed "Chew and Release." "Chew and Release" usually works like this: first, I look to see if we have a parental unit present. If so, I look for the attitude of mom or dad. Mom or dad present, I try to read facial expressions and body language to see if the court is being used, as it should be, as a threat and a consequence. Next, I gauge the level of fear and contrition in the young person's attitude. Most are unnerved by being in court, so the task is easy. With a serious look on my face and a stern voice, I demand a plea. Usually we get a guilty. Then we move into the lecture on what a life of crime can lead to and the deadbeat existence that awaits them at the end of this course of conduct. When the acceptable level of contrition is demonstrated, the court orders a sentence of parole with a threat of dire consequences and punishment if I ever see the offender in court again.

The "Release" is next in sequence. The experience not having been much fun, youngsters are eager to leave, so when released, they make a beeline for the exit. Frequently, as I make eye contact with the parents, they nod in approval and occasionally will silently mouth the words "thank you." If the young malefactors are not contrite or remorseful, the "Chew" part of the process escalates and continues until we see regret and remorse, or the alternative, fear, on their divine little faces. Once the appropriate attitude has been achieved, parole is sternly imposed and we are ready for the "Release."

Occasionally when these youngsters are released, I have an almost overwhelming urge to break into a chorus of "Born Free" as they bolt for the exit. They are once again free to run amok in the neighborhoods and school grounds.

The "Chew and Release" program has been very effective. In over sixteen years, I can recall only two repeat offenders and no three-time losers. I heard from a sixth grade teacher at the local grade school who overheard a conversation that included one of his students who had appeared in court the night before. The youngster said with great conviction that the judge was scary and mean. Ah, the power of a scowl and a stern voice.

So, on to the night at issue. While reviewing the docket before court on this particular evening, I was advised by the clerk that there were three candidates for the "Chew and Release" program. That is all that was said, but by the tone of her voice, the clerk clearly had a greater understanding of the events and history than I did and seemed to anticipate the appearances with some degree of enthusiasm. So, now I was curious.

As court begins, I note three young lads sitting together. By their appearance and attitudes, one can tell that they think they are tough. Real tough for ten- or eleven-year-olds. Only one child seems to have a parent with him and one in particular is clearly the toughest of the tough kids. The ringleader, as it were. As court begins, they continue to whisper, point at me and the police officers, and laugh and snicker. Clearly, they are unimpressed by the institution and the forum they are appearing in.

As we work our way through the docket, we eventually

get to the first of the three citations for the tough kids. "Mr. Bigstuff," the court calls out. The fates are with us this evening—the toughest of the tough stands. He nods to his two sidekicks, gives them a thumbs-up sign, and begins a slow swagger as he moves toward the bench. So, here he is. Four feet something tall, a little stocky for his diminutive size, shaggy and messy hair. Wearing a red flannel plaid shirt with the sleeves cut out at the shoulder. The shirt, of course, is not tucked into his pants. Baggy jeans and sneakers; untied sneakers, of course. Oh yeah, we mustn't forget the shirt is unbuttoned halfway down, revealing a hairless chest and chain around his neck. He is chewing gum with his mouth open and a smirk on his face. So much bravado for such a small package. When he gets to the appointed spot he stops, puts his hands on his hips, chewing his gum, head bobbing as he looks around, and glances back at his cohorts to be sure they are watching. The cohorts nod and smile with great approval. And then we make eye contact, and the engagement begins.

"Mr. Bigstuff, you are appearing on two citations. The first is for failure to wear a bicycle helmet, and the second is for a curfew violation. How do you plead?"

He has to bob his head a couple of times, chew on his gum, and smirk a little more, and then he answers, "I don't see why I should have to wear a helmet."

"Mr. Bigstuff, we are not here to debate the validity of the law. You are appearing here for your first appearance for these two citations. I need a plea from you of guilty, not guilty, or no contest. If you are not sure what those options mean, I can explain them to you."

"Naw, I get it," he responds. "I did not have a helmet on, so I guess I will just plead guilty."

"And on the curfew violation, how to you plead?"

"Well, it was kind of late, so I guess I will plead guilty on that one, too."

With a guilty plea, I take a moment to review the police report that is in the packet. As suspected, the report lists several encounters with the officer involving both helmet and curfew issues. The curfew that is the basis for this citation is for 1:30 AM. Curfew for children of this age is 9:00 PM in this jurisdiction. So now the Chew begins. Scowl on face, stern voice, medium volume.

"Mr. Bigstuff, I can see from the officer's report that this is not the first time the officer had spoken to you about not wearing a bicycle helmet."

"Yeah, he has caught me before."

"Do you have a helmet?"

"Nope," he smirks with a laugh.

"The officer offered you a helmet, didn't he?"

"Yeah, but I don't want one, and I wouldn't wear it if I had one."

"How about the curfew violation? Why were you so late?"

"We were just hanging out. We weren't doing nothing. We weren't bothering nobody. So, what's the big deal?"

With those wise-guy remarks and a negative attitude that is not only continuing, but increasing, the Chew needs to escalate. So, leaning forward, more scowl, louder voice, I launch forth.

"Mr. Bigstuff, there are and will be many laws or rules that you do not agree with or understand. However, our society does not work on the principle of everyone doing what they think they want to do. We have the laws and the rules that we all have to follow and when we don't, we end up where you are right now: in front of a judge, looking at a fine or a penalty of some sort."

By his expression, which has not changed from the smirk he started with, I can tell that we have not yet made an impression on the lad. So, on we go with more Chew and more intensity on my part.

"This is a very important lesson for you to learn at this point in your life. If you think you can ignore the rules society imposes on all of us, you will end up in juvenile detention and ultimately in prison. There you will have to do exactly what you are told to do when you are told to do it."

Still no impact. There he stands. Flaunting his arrogance in the belief that there is nothing anyone can do to him. But failure is not an option, especially when I see the two cohorts. They are grinning and enjoying Mr. Bigstuff's performance and anticipating their turns at being insolent and disrespectful. I am thinking that I have a pretty good understanding of what the officer's experience has been which has resulted in Mr. Bigstuff's appearance here tonight. What we have here is a war of wills. And this is a war I will not lose. This being a new experience for me, not having met such a challenge from such a young person, I need time to consider alternatives. Fortunately, I have a foolproof method of buying time. So, on with the battle.

"Mr. Bigstuff, I can see that you are not taking this matter seriously. This is all a big joke to you, isn't it?"

He nods vigorously in agreement. Once again, the look

over his shoulder to the cohort duo, who are grinning back with great approval.

"Mr. Bigstuff, I am going to take you into custody while I decide what to do with you. Officer, please take the defendant into custody and remove him from the courtroom."

Suddenly, the smirk and attitude neutralizes. A look of curiosity or confusion now appears. The officer gladly steps forward behind Mr. Bigstuff and asks him to put his hands behind his back. Now shocked with disbelief, he actually complies. It takes a moment for the handcuffs to be appropriately fastened and checked. The courtroom is silent. You literally could hear a pin drop. The officer asks Mr. Bigstuff if he has any weapons, knives, or razorblades, or anything that will hurt or injure the officer as he pats Mr. Bigstuff down and checks his pockets. Mr. Bigstuff answers in what is a now more childlike voice, "No."

The reality of what has happened just now fully sinks in for the young man. He has lost control of the situation. The smirk is gone. The cocky attitude is replaced with concern. As he is led from the courtroom, he is looking pleadingly at the two cohorts, who have nothing to offer in assistance other than to stare in amazement as the toughest of them all is led from the courtroom and the door from which he exits closes ominously behind him. And then he is gone. The events dramatically change the two cohort's countenances also.

We intentionally hesitate for a long moment to let the impact of the moment settle in on the crowd. And it does.

Then on we go with court. More cases are called. Pleas accepted. Fines imposed. Trial dates set. And so on and so on. Then we come to the first of the two junior tough-guy cohorts.

Strangely, what approaches the bench when Mr. Tagalong's name is called is a timid, scared little boy about ten years old. Tough kid is no longer present. Guilty pleas are entered and accepted. The Chew is firm and direct. Parole for the rest of his juvenile life is imposed with a promise that if he ever appears before me again, he will regret it. When the Release is finally offered, Mr. Tagalong's departure from the courtroom is as expeditious as those short little legs can carry him.

A few names later on the docket, we get to the last of the Three Delinquenteers. Mr. Tagalongalso repeats the performance of Mr. Tagalong, so I repeat my performance also. Seems fair. Right? Upon Release, Mr. Tagalongalso is visibly restraining himself from running as he walks quickly from the courtroom.

Court continues on through the docket, pay-or-appears, and trials. When all is done, I inquire as to the status of Mr. Bigstuff. The officer advises he has been behaving very nicely while detained. I request that he be returned to the courtroom.

When Mr. Bigstuff comes back, he is a changed boy. We all learn an interesting fact that evening. When your hands are restrained behind your back by handcuffs, you cannot wipe the tears away as they run down your face. It is hard to maintain that tough-guy image with tear stains on your cheeks. Not even the chain around his neck can overcome this chink in the tough-guy armor. But this is no time to ease up; one must strike while the iron is hot. And this iron seems to be red hot.

"Mr. Bigstuff, I am going to give you one more chance. Your arrogant, insolent attitude (words I doubt he understands other than to know that they are not complimentary) will not be tolerated in this court. Do you understand me?"

"Yes, sir," he replies with a great deal of contrition.

Aw, there it was. The attitude we were looking for. Success at last.

"Mr. Bigstuff, if I release you tonight, you will be required to come to the police station tomorrow morning to pick out a bicycle helmet for yourself. They have several to choose from. Will you do that?"

"I don't need a helmet. I have one at home," he confesses.

"Then you are going to have to wear it whenever you are on your or anyone else's bike. Do you understand that?"

"Yes."

"Will you do it?

"Yes," he states with some conviction.

"Now, for the curfew issue. Curfew for this jurisdiction is 9:00 PM. Do you understand that?"

Once again, a convincing "Yes."

"Mr. Bigstuff, your attitude when you came to court and when we first talked is not acceptable. From reading the police report, it appears that it is the same attitude you have used with the police officers. That also is not acceptable and will not be tolerated. Do you understand me?"

"Yes," now almost a whimper.

"If I release you tonight and put you on parole until you are eighteen years old, will you promise me that I will never see you back in this court again?"

He now sees a ray of hope and anxiously replies, "You will never see me back here again. I promise! I promise!"

"Very well. I will give you just this one more chance. I will release you based on your word and your promise that you will be wearing that helmet whenever you are on or near a bike and will not be out without an adult after curfew. Are we clear on that?"

"You bet. I will do that."

"Officer, please remove the handcuffs from Mr. Bigstuff."

While the handcuffs are being removed, hope returns to Mr. Bigstuff. The anticipation of going home, or at least out of where he is, and the yearning for freedom are more than a hope. The few seconds it takes to remove the police-issued personal jewelry seem like minutes to the boy. Apparently, he has itches that need to be rubbed, or feels compelled to inventory his anatomy, because once the cuffs are off, he rubs or touches various parts of himself. However, none that are inappropriate in public.

Once he has composed himself, I once again address the young man.

"Mr. Bigstuff, curfew starts in about thirty-five minutes, so as you leave us this evening you should go directly home. You are now free to go."

No more need to be said. He was moving deliberately and diligently toward the exit door and had disappeared into the night long before the door could gracefully close.

I never saw Mr. Bigstuff, Mr. Tagalong, or Mr. Tagalongalso again. I have no idea if the experience had any impact on their young lives. But at least for a few moments one evening, the recognition of an institution that could deliver a consequence delivered on its promise. Being the eternal optimist that I am, I am betting that they all turned out OK.

A Short Primer on Municipal Court Procedures

I N THE WORLD OF COURTS of law, somewhere in the realm of things largely ignored, there is what is known in our jurisdiction as the municipal court. Municipal courts primarily handle misdemeanors, traffic violations, and ordinance violations. While the services provided by the court are certainly important to the peace and tranquility of the good citizens, "muni" court deals with that section of the spectrum of civil misconduct that is less serious than murder, assault, battery, forgery, and arson. So, the deeds of the malefactors also tend to be, oh, shall we say, more misguided than truly evil. While the conduct may be premeditated, it is more like "red-necked" than "white-collared."

In small towns such as those in which I have served, financial resources are limited, and it then follows that all other resources, including human resources, are limited. By definition, small towns have small populations. Thus, they have small tax bases with lower revenue, fewer services, facilities, and amenities—you get the idea. Thus, the two jurisdictions in which I have served can afford only a part-time magistrate (me) and do not have a dedicated courtroom.

Court is scheduled two or three times a month, usually in the evening. Evening court, some would call it night court, is offered so as to make court time available during an hour when presumably most people will not be working. If people are not at work, they are more likely to come to court. Moreover, the city itself is able to staff that time with both court-clerk staff and police-officer support and utilize space that is being used during normal business hours. We have held court in city council chambers, in recreation halls, at the grange hall, and in a playhouse (where thespians perform, not a diminutive house for small children or dolls).

We are not a court of record. There is no court reporter to transcribe everything that is said in the courtroom, nor are the proceedings recorded. We are not a court of last resort, meaning an appeal can be made from municipal court to the county court where there is a full-time judge, a jury, a dedicated courtroom with the traditional marble, oak, mahogany—you get the picture. However, the filing fee in county court for an appeal is almost as high as most minimum fines in muni court; therefore, very few appeals are ever filed.

While not cloaked with the mystique and reverence of the Supreme Court, and lacking the institutional dignity that accompanies a full-time staff, juries, and the like, municipal courts nonetheless contribute to the overall stability of the community by enforcing local ordinances and addressing the non-felony matters that are considered more irritating than serious criminal acts. Although the offenses are not as severe in nature, these "irritants" tend to be committed by and affect a greater number of citizens. Simply put, municipal courts fill a slot in the court system that administers justice and thereby helps to keep the peace.

In municipal court, we deal with traffic tickets, lots of traffic tickets. We deal with barking dogs, dogs at large, theft of services, junk in your yard, too many junk cars in your yard, junk cars parked on the street, pedestrian violations, shoplifting, theft (the little one without the use of weapons or breaking and entering), loud noise, and so on.

So, how does one end up in muni court? Individuals are cited by police officers or public officials to appear in municipal court. This is accomplished by issuing them what is commonly known as a "ticket" or more formally known as a citation. The ticket will "cite" them to appear in court on a specific date and time. Or, for the convenience of the individual cited, there are write-in options on the back of his or her copy of the ticket. One can admit guilt or plead no contest, post the bail that is written on the face of the ticket, and submit an explanation to the court. The court will accept a guilty or a no-contest plea, review a letter if one is submitted, and then impose a penalty as allowed or required by law, thus eliminating the need for the individual to appear in court. Very efficient, right? However, most people do not avail themselves of this convenience. The courtroom is never lacking for those who want to have their day and say in court. In choosing to exercise their right to tell their side of the story, they have unwittingly provided the material for this book.

So into court they come. Some are humorous. Some are in a bad mood. Some feign ignorance, while others truly are ignorant. Some pretend brilliance and intellect. Some beg for mercy. Some claim to have repented of their misguided ways and pledge faithful compliance to all laws of man and nature until the end of time. Some try to schmooze their way out of the citation. Some try to play lawyer. And some try to intimidate the court. Why, you might ask. I have never figured that out. I have police officers with guns and handcuffs; they have their foul mouths and glaring looks. Go figure.

Individuals cited into court will appear at what is referred to as a first appearance. Kind of an obvious name since this will, in fact, be the first time the individual appears in court for that ticket. At the first appearance, the individual will respond to the charge by entering a plea. There are three options: guilty, no contest, and not guilty.

A guilty plea is an admission of guilt. If an individual enters a guilty plea, the court then allows the individual to explain extraordinary or unusual circumstances that may warrant consideration in the disposition of the citation. This informs and assists the court in the imposition of a reasonable, and hopefully just, penalty.

A no-contest plea basically says it is not worth fighting this, but I do not want to admit I was wrong. While technically and legally different, the result is the same as a guilty plea: an opportunity to explain, followed by imposition of a fine.

Now, then, a not-guilty plea is different. A not-guilty plea results in a trial. The officer who issued or served the citation and, if the citation is signed by a citizen, the citizen who signed the citation are required to appear and testify under oath to the facts that establish the legal elements necessary to prove the allegations of the citation. Stated differently, the city has to prove the case against the defendant before the defendant has to utter a word in his or her own defense. However, due to the nature of the type of citations, those facts are generally and readily available and therefore easily proven.

The defendant is then given an opportunity to present any evidence, including his or her own sworn testimony, the testimony of witnesses, or any demonstrative evidence in support of the defense. The city is then allowed an opportunity to rebut that evidence. Thereafter, the court will weigh the evidence and enter a finding. A finding of not guilty results in a dismissal, whereas a finding of guilty results in the imposition of a penalty or a fine.

Penalties in municipal court are limited to a slap in the pocketbook (i.e., we take your hard-earned or ill-gotten money). At the beginning of court, a city ordinance is recited, putting everyone on notice that they are subject to fine or forfeiture (i.e., money); there is no other civil penalty for the violation for which they are appearing. So, the penalty will be a fine and not jail time. There are, however, two exceptions to the promise not to send anyone to jail. The first exception is for not appearing in court as scheduled. One to two reminder letters will be sent, and if they are ignored, the court will issue a warrant for failure to appear. The second scenario is for failing to pay a fine that has been ordered or for failing to appear in court to explain why a previously imposed fine has not been paid as scheduled. Thus, a warrant will be issued for failure to pay the fine.

Our county jail is like most jails. It is overcrowded. There is a maximum capacity limitation that cannot be exceeded, at least not after about 9:00 AM of each day. Except this "cap," as it is referred to, is not required on the weekends. So, if an individual is lodged on a municipal court warrant, he or she may have the pleasure of spending the weekend in jail at most or, more likely, a single, long, lonely night away from the company of his/her loved ones. The intent of the warrant and the threat of being lodged in jail is not intended as a penalty for the violation of an ordinance or a law. Rather, it is intended to get people's attention and encourage them to meet their civic obligation of appearing in court when ordered, or availing themselves of the preferred option, which is the traditional paying of the fine. And with all candor, I must say it has been very effective.

There it is. Short as promised. Intended to provide the reader with a basic understanding of the processes in muni court and also to help the reader understand the context in which the events describe in this book take place. And, no, you are not now a lawyer because you read these few paragraphs. So all the lawyer jokes do not apply to you.